T0178803

Memory Allocation Problems in Embedded Systems

Memory Allocation Problems in Embedded Systems

Optimization Methods

María Soto
André Rossi
Marc Sevaux
Johann Laurent

Series Editor

Narendra Jussien

First published 2013 in Great Britain and the United States by ISTE Ltd and John Wiley & Sons, Inc.

ISTE Ltd
27-37 St George's Road
London SW19 4EU
UK

www.iste.co.uk

John Wiley & Sons, Inc.
111 River Street
Hoboken, NJ 07030
USA

www.wiley.com

© ISTE Ltd 2013

The rights of María Soto, André Rossi, Marc Sevaux and Johann Laurent to be identified as the author of this work have been asserted by them in accordance with the Copyright, Designs and Patents Act 1988.

Library of Congress Control Number: 2012951962

British Library Cataloguing-in-Publication Data
A CIP record for this book is available from the British Library
ISBN: 978-1-84821-428-6

Printed and bound in Great Britain by CPI Group (UK) Ltd., Croydon, Surrey CR0 4YY

Table of Contents

Introduction

This book addresses four memory allocation problems. The following sections present the motivations, the main contributions and the outline of this book.

Motivations

Embedded systems are ever present in contemporary society and they are supposed to make our lives more comfortable. In industry, embedded systems are used to manage and control complex systems (e.g. nuclear power plants, telecommunication, and flight control; they are also playing an important role in our daily activities (e.g. smartphones, security alarms and traffic lights).

The significant development in embedded systems is mainly due to advances in nano technology. These continuous advances have made possible the design of miniaturized electronic chips, leading to drastically extend the features supported by embedded systems. Smartphones that can surf the Web and process HD images are a typical example. In addition to market pressure, this context has favored the development of computer-aided design (CAD) software, which brings a greater change to the designer's line of work. While technology offers more and more opportunities, the design of embedded systems becomes more and more complex. Indeed, the design of an integrated circuit, whose size is calculated in billions of transistors, thousands of memories, etc., requires the use of competitive computer tools. These tools have to solve optimization problems to ensure a low cost in terms of area and time, and they must meet some standards in electronics.

Currently, in the electronics industry, the problems are often addressed using either *ad hoc* methods based on the designer expertise or general methods (typically genetic algorithms). But both methods do not work well in solving large-scale industrial problems.

On the other hand, computer-aided design software such as Gaut [GAU 93, COU 06] has been developed to generate the architecture of a chip (circuit) from its specifications. While the design process is significantly faster with these types of software, the generated layouts are considered to be poor on power consumption and surface compared to man-made expertly-designed circuits. This is a major drawback as embedded products have to feature low-power consumption.

In the design of embedded systems, memory allocation and data assignment are among the main challenges that electronic designers have to face. Indeed, they deeply impact on the main cost metrics (power consumption, performance and area) in electronic devices [WUY 96]. Thus, designers of embedded system have to carefully pay attention to minimize memory requirements, improving memory throughput and limiting the power consumption by the system's memory. Electronic designers attempt to minimize memory requirements with the aim of lowering the overall system costs.

Moreover, the need for optimization of the allocation of data structures is expected to become even more stringent in the future, as embedded systems will run heavy computations. As an example, some cell phones already support multi-threading operating systems.

For these reasons, we are interested in the allocation of data structures into memory banks. This problem is rather difficult to handle and is often left to the compiler with which automatic rules are applied. Nevertheless, an optimal allocation of data to memory banks may lead to greater savings in terms of running time and energy consumption.

As has often been observed in microelectronics, this complex problem is poorly modeled or not modeled at all. The proposed solutions are based on a lower modeling level that often only considers one objective at a time. Also, the optimization of methods is little (or not) quantified, only the running time is available and assessed. Thus, the models and data are not analyzed much.

In this book, we model this problem and propose optimization methods from operations research for addressing it.

Contribution

In memory management and data assignment, there is an abundant literature on the techniques for optimizing source code and for designing a good architecture for an application. However, not much work looks at finding a good allocation of data structure to memory banks. Hence, the first contribution of this book is the introduction of four versions of memory allocation problems, which are either related to designing the memory architecture or focused on the data structure assignment.

The second important contribution of this book is the introduction of three new upper bounds on the chromatic number without making any assumption on the graph structure. These uppers bounds are used to address our first memory allocation problem.

The third contribution is the design of exact mathematical models and metaheuristic approaches to address these versions of the memory allocation problem. Additionally, the proposed metaheuristics are compared with exact methods on a large set of instances.

Finally, in order to achieve this work, we have undertaken some challenges between operations research and electronics. Thus, this book aims at contributing to reducing the gap between these two fields and these two communities.

Outline

The problems addressed in this book are presented by increasing complexity, with the aim of smoothly introducing the reader to these problems; each version of the memory allocation problem is separately developed in different chapters. This book is organized as follows:

– Chapter 1 describes the general context in which this work has been conducted. We highlight the strong dependence of contemporary society on embedded systems. A state of the art of optimization techniques for memory management and data assignment is presented. We discuss the benefits of using operations research for electronic design.

– Chapter 2 presents the first version of the memory allocation problem. The work presented in this chapter has been presented in detail [SOT 09], and was published in the journal *Discrete Applied* Mathematics.

– Chapter 3 deals with the second version of the memory allocation problem. This is the allocation of data structures into memory banks while making minimum hypotheses on the targeted chip. The main characteristic in the memory architecture is that the number of memory banks is fixed. The work around this problem has been published as a long article in Roadef 2010 [SOT 10].

– Chapter 4 addresses the general memory allocation problem. This problem is more realistic than the previous problem; in addition to memory banks, an *external memory* is considered in the target architecture. Moreover, more constraints on memory banks and data structures are considered. The work about the general memory allocation problem has been published in the *Journal of Heuristics* [SOT 11a].

– Chapter 5 deals with the last version of the memory allocation problem. This problem is concerned with dynamic memory allocation; it has a special emphasis on time performance. A memory allocation must consider the requirement and constraints at each time interval, that is it can be adjusted to the application needs at each time interval. This problem has been presented at EVOCOP 2011 [SOT 11c].

– Chapter 6 presents a general conclusion to this work; it discusses results and provides ideas for future work.

– Chapter 7 discusses the implementation of this work in a software called *Softexplorer*. It is available free at http://www.softexplorer.fr/.

Chapter 1

Context

This chapter describes the general context in which this work has been conducted, how our work takes its roots and how this research can be placed in the field of electronic design.

In section 1.1 of this chapter, we highlight the importance nowadays of embedded systems. Section 1.2 stresses the relationship between memory management and three relevant cost metrics (such as power consumption, area and performance) in embedded systems. This explains the considerable amount of research carried out in the field of memory management. Then, the following section presents a brief survey of the state of the art in optimization techniques for memory management, and, at the same time, positions our work with respect to the aforementioned techniques. Finally, operations research for electronic design is taken into consideration for examining the mutual benefits of both disciplines and the main challenges exploiting operations research methods to electronic problems.

1.1. Embedded systems

There are many definitions for embedded systems in the literature (for instance [HEA 03], [BAR 06], [KAM 08] and [NOE 05]) but they all converge toward the same point: "An embedded system is a minicomputer (microprocessor-based) system designed to control one specific function or a range of functions; but, it is not designed to be programmed by the end user in the same way that a personal computer (PC) is".

A PC is built to be flexible and to meet a wide range of end user needs. Thus, the user can change the functionality of the system by adding or replacing software, for example one minute the PC is a video game platform and the next minute it can be used as a video player. In contrast, the embedded system was originally designed so that the end user could make choices regarding the different application options, but could not change the functionality of the system by adding software. However, nowadays, this distinction is less and less relevant; for example it is more frequent to find smartphones where we can change their functionality by installing appropriate software. In this manner, the breach between a PC and an embedded system is shorter today than it was in the past.

An embedded system can be a complete electronic device or a part of an application or component within a larger system. This explains its wide range of applicability. Embedded systems range from portable devices such as digital watches to large stationary installations such as systems controlling nuclear power plants.

Indeed, depending on application, an embedded system can monitor temperature, time, pressure, light, sound, movement or button sensitivity (like on Apple iPods).

We can find embedded systems helping us in every day common tasks; for example alarm clocks, smartphones, security alarms, TV remote controls, MP3 players and traffic lights. Not to mention modern cars and trucks that contain many embedded systems: one embedded system controls the antilock brakes, another monitors and controls the vehicle's emissions and a third displays information in the dashboard [BAR 06].

Besides, embedded systems are present on real-time systems. The main characteristic of these kinds of systems is timing constraints. A real-time system must be able to make some calculations or decisions in a timely manner knowing that these important calculations or activities have deadlines for completion [BAR 06]. Real-time systems can be found in telecommunications, factory controllers, flight control and electronic engines. Not forgetting, the real-time multi-dimensional signal processing (RMSP) domain that includes applications, like video and image processing, medical imaging, artificial vision, real-time 3D rendering, advanced audio and speech coding recognition [CAT 98b].

Contemporary society, or industrial civilization, is strongly dependent on embedded systems. They are around us simplifying our tasks and pretending to make our life more comfortable.

1.1.1. *Main components of embedded systems*

Generally, an embedded system is mainly composed of a processor, a memory, peripherals and software. Below, we give a brief explanation of these components.

− *Processor*: this should provide the processing power needed to perform the tasks within the system. This main criterion for the processor seems obvious but it frequently occurs that the tasks are either underestimated in terms of their size and/or complexity or that creeping elegance[1] expands the specification beyond the processor's capability [HEA 03].

− *Memory*: this depends on how the software is designed, written and developed. Memory is an important part of any embedded system design and has two essential functions: it provides storage for the software that will be run, and it provides storage for data, such as program variables, intermediate results, status information and any other data created when the application runs [HEA 03].

− *Peripherals*: these allow an embedded system to communicate with the outside world. Sensors that measure the external environment are typical examples of input peripherals [HEA 03].

− *Software*: this defines what an embedded system does and how well it does it. For example, an embedded application can interpret information from external sensors by adopting algorithms for modeling external environments. Software encompasses the technology that adds value to the system.

In this work, we are interested in the management of embedded system memory. Consequently, the other embedded system components are not addressed here. The next section justifies this choice.

1.2. Memory management for decreasing power consumption, performance and area in embedded systems

Embedded systems are very cost sensitive and in practice, the system designers implement their applications on the

---

1 Creeping elegance is the tendency of programmers to disproportionately emphasize elegance in software at the expense of other requirements such as functionality, shipping schedule and usability.

basis of "cost" measures, such as the number of components, performance, pin count, power consumption and the area of the custom components. In previous years, the main focus has been on area-efficient designs. In fact, most research in digital electronics has focused on increasing the speed and integration of digital systems on a chip while keeping the silicon area as small as possible. As a result, the design technology is powerful but power hungry. While focusing on speed and area, power consumption has long been ignored [CAT 98b].

However, this situation has changed during the last decade mainly due to the increasing demand for handheld devices in the areas of communication (e.g. smartphones), computation (e.g. personal digital assistants) and consumer electronics (e.g. multimedia terminals and digital video cameras). All these portable systems require sophisticated and power-hungry algorithms for high-bandwidth wireless communication, video-compression and -decompression, handwriting recognition, speech processing and so on. Portable systems without low-power design suffer from either a very short battery life or an unreasonably heavy battery. This higher power consumption also means more costly packaging, cooling equipment and lower reliability. The latter is a major problem for many high-performance applications; thus, power-efficient design is a crucial point in the design of a broad class of applications [RAB 02, CAT 98b].

Lower power design requires optimizations at all levels of the design hierarchy, for example technology, device, circuit, logic, architecture, algorithm and system level [CHA 95, RAB 02].

Memory design for multi-processor and embedded systems has always been a crucial issue because system-level performance strongly depends on memory organization. Embedded systems are often designed under stringent energy consumption budgets to limit heat generation and battery size. Because memory systems consume a significant amount of energy to store and to forward data, it is then imperative to balance (trade-off) energy consumption and performance in memory design [MAC 05].

The RMSP domain and the network component domain are typical examples of data-dominated applications[2]. For data-dominated applications, a very large part of the power consumption is due to data storage and data transfer. Indeed, a lot of memory is needed to store the data processed; and huge amounts of data are transfered back and forth between the memories and data paths[3]. Also, the area cost is heavily impacted by memory organization [CAT 98b].

Figure 1.1, taken from [CAT 98b], shows that data transfers and memory access operations consume much more power than a data-path operation in both cases: hardware and software implementations. In the context of a typical heterogeneous system architecture, which is illustrated in Figure 1.2 (taken from [CAT 98b]), this architecture disposes of custom hardware, programmable software and a distributed memory organization that is frequently costly in terms of power and area. We can estimate that downloading an operand from off-chip memory for a multiplication consumes approximately 33 times more power than the multiplication itself for the hardware processor. Hence, in the case of a multiplication with two factors where the result is stored in the off-chip memory, the power consumption of transferring

---

2 Data-dominated applications are so named like this because they process enormous amounts of data.

3 Data-path is a collection of functional units, such as arithmetic logic units or multipliers, that perform data processing operations. A functional unit is a part of a central processing unit (CPU) that performs the operations and calculations called by the computer program.

data is approximately 100 times more than the actual computation.

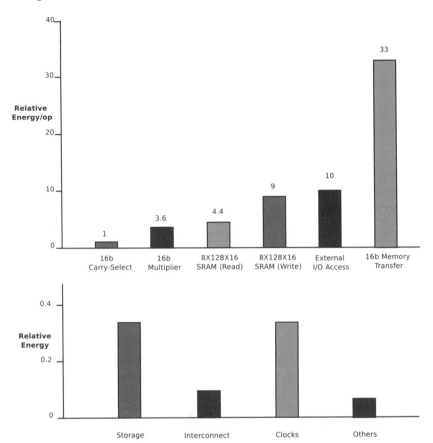

Figure 1.1. *Dominance of transfer and storage over data-path operation both in hardware and software*

Furthermore, studies presented in [CAT 94], [MEN 95], [NAC 96], [TIW 94] and [GON 96] confirm that data transfer and storage dominates power consumption for data-dominated applications in hardware and software implementations.

In the context of memory organization design, there are two strategies for minimizing the power consumption in embedded systems. The first strategy is to reduce the energy consumed in accessing memories. This takes a dominant proportion of the energy budget of an embedded system for data-dominated applications. The second strategy is to minimize the amount of energy consumed when information is exchanged between the processor and the memory. It reduces the amount of required processor-to-memory communication bandwidth [MAC 05].

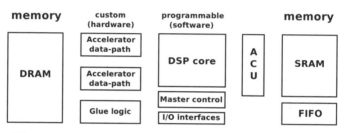

Figure 1.2. *Typical heterogeneous embedded architecture*

1.3. State of the art in optimization techniques for memory management and data assignment

It is clear that memory management has an impact on important cost metrics: area, performance and power consumption. In fact, the processor cores begin to push the limits of high performance, and the gap between processor and memory widens and usually becomes the bottleneck in achieving high performance. Hence, the designers of embedded systems have to carefully pay attention to minimize memory requirements, improve memory throughput and limit the power consumption by the system's memory. Thus, the designer attempts to minimize memory requirements with the aim of lowering overall system costs.

We distinguish three problems concerning memory management and data assignment. The first problem is software oriented and aims at optimizing application code source regardless of the architecture; it is called a software optimization and it is presented in section 1.3.1. In the second problem, the electronic designer searches for the best architecture in terms of cost metrics for a specific embedded application. This problem is described in section 1.3.2. In the third problem, the designer is concerned with binding the application data into memory in a fixed architecture so as to minimize power consumption. This problem is presented in section 1.3.3.

1.3.1. *Software optimization*

We present some global optimizations that are independent of the target architectural platform; readers interested in more details about this are refereed to [PAN 01b]. These optimization techniques take the form of source-to-source code transformations. This has a positive effect on the area consumption by reducing the amount of data transfers and/or the amount of data to be stored. Software optimization often improves performances cost and power consumption, but not always. They are important in finding the best alternatives in higher levels of the embedded system design.

Code-rewriting techniques consist of loop and data-flow transformations with the aim of reducing the required amount of data transfer and storage, and improving access behavior [CAT 01]. The goal of global data-flow transformation is to reduce the number of bottlenecks in the algorithm and remove access redundancy in the data flow. This consists of avoiding unnecessary copies of data, modifying computation order, shifting of "delay lines" through the algorithm to reduce the storage requirements and recomputing issues to reduce the number of transfers and storage size [CAT 98a]. Basically, global loop and control-flow transformations increase the locality and regularity of the code's accesses. This is clearly good for memory size (area) and memory accesses (power) [FRA 94] but of course also for performance [MAS 99]. In addition, global loop and control-flow transformations reduce the global life-times of the variables. This removes system-level copy overhead in buffers and enables storing data in smaller memories closer to the data paths [DEG 95, KOL 94].

The *hierarchical memory organization* is a memory optimization technique (see [BEN 00c] for a list of references). It reduces memory energy by exploiting the non-uniformities in access frequencies to instructions and data [HEN 07]. This technique consists of placing frequently accessed data into small energy-efficient memories, while rarely accessed information is stored in large memories with high cost per access. The energy cost of accessing and communicating with the small memories is much smaller than the cost required to fetch and store information in large memories [BEN 00a, CUP 98].

A good way for decreasing the memory traffic, as well as memory energy, is to *compress the information* transmitted between two levels of memory hierarchy [MAC 05]. This technique consists of choosing the set of data elements to be compressed/decompressed and the time instants during execution at which these compressions or decompressions should be performed [OZT 09]. The memory bottlenecks are mainly due to the increasing code complexity of embedded applications and the exponential increase in the amount of data to manipulate. Hence, reducing the memory-space occupancy of embedded applications is very important. For this reason, designers and researchers have devised techniques for improving the code density (code compression), in terms of speed, area and energy [BAJ 97]. Data compression techniques have been introduced in [BEN 02a, BEN 02b].

Ordering and bandwidth optimization guarantees that the real-time constraints are presented with a minimal memory bandwidth-related costs. Also, this determines which data should be made simultaneously accessible in the memory architecture.

Moreover, storage-bandwidth optimization takes into account the effect on power dissipation. The data that are dominant in terms of power consumption are split into smaller pieces of data. Indeed, allocating more and smaller memories usually results in less power consumption; but the use of this technique is limited by the additional costs generated by routing overheads, extra design effort and more extensive testing in the design [SLO 97].

This chapter does not cover optimization techniques on source code transformation. It is focused on optimization techniques on hardware and on data binding in an existing memory architecture.

1.3.2. *Hardware optimization*

We now present some techniques for optimizing the memory architecture design of embedded systems.

The goal of *memory allocation and data assignment* is to determine an optimal memory architecture for data structures of a specific application. This decides the memory parameters, such as the number and the capacity of memories and the number of ports in each memory. Different choices can lead to solutions with a very different cost, which emphasize how important these choices are. The freedom of the memory architecture is constrained by the requirements of the application. Allocating more or less memories has an effect on the chip area and on the energy consumption of the memory architecture. Large memories consume more energy per access than small memories, because of longer word – and bit – lines. So the energy consumed by a single large memory containing all the data is much larger than when the data are distributed over several smaller memories. Moreover, the area of a single memory solution is often higher when different arrays have different bit widths [PAN 01b].

For convenience and with the aim of producing sophisticated solutions, memory allocation and assignment is subdivided into two subproblems (a systematic technique has been published for the two subproblems in [SLO 97], [CAT 98c] and [LIP 93]). The first subproblem consists of fixing the number of memories and the type of each of them. The term "type" includes the number of access ports of the memory, whether it is an on-chip or an off-chip memory. The second subproblem decides in which of the allocated memories each of the application's array (data) will be stored. Hence, the dimensions of the memories are determined by the characteristics of the data assigned to each memory and it is possible to estimate the memory cost. The cost of memory architecture depends on the word-length (bits) and the number of words of each memory, and the number of times each of the memories is accessed. Using this cost estimation, it is possible to explore different alternative assignment schemes and select the best one for implementation [CAT 98b]. The search space can be explored using either a greedy constructive heuristic or a full-search branch and bound approach [CAT 98b]. For small applications, branch and bound method and integer linear programming (ILP) find optimal solutions, but if the size of the application gets larger, these algorithms take a huge computation time to generate an optimal solution.

For one-port (write/read) memories, memory allocation and assignment problems can be modeled as a *vertex coloring problem* [GAR 79]. In this conflict graph, a variable is represented by a vertex, a memory is represented by a color and an edge is present between two conflicting variables. Thus, the variable of the application is "colored" with the memories to which they are assigned. Two variables in conflict cannot have the same color [CAT 98b]. This model is also used for assigning scalars to registers. With multi port memories, the conflict graph has to be extended with loops and hyperedges and an ordinary coloring is not valid anymore.

The objective of *in-place mapping* optimization is to find the optimal placement of the data inside the memories such that the required memory capacity is minimal [DEG 97, VER 91]. The goal of this strategy is to reuse memory location as much as possible and hence reduce the storage size requirements. This means that several data entities can be stored at the same location at different times. There are two subproblems: the intra-array storage and inter-array storage [CAT 98b]. The intra-array storage refers to the internal organization of an array in memory [LUI 07b, TRO 02]. The inter-array storage refers to the relative position of different arrays in memory [LUI 07a]. Balasa *et al.* [BAL 08] give a tutorial overview on the existing techniques for the evaluation of the data memory size.

A *data transfer and storage exploration methodology* is a technique for simultaneous optimization of memory architecture and access patterns. It has also been proposed for the case of data-dominated applications (e.g. multimedia devices) and network component applications (e.g. Automated Teller Machine applications) [CAT 98b, BRO 00, CAT 94, CAT 98a, WUY 96]. The goal of this methodology is to determine an optimal execution order for the data transfer and an optimal memory architecture for storing the data of a given application. The steps in this methodology are decoupled and placed in a specific order, which reduces the number of iterations between the steps and shortens the overall design time. These steps are:

- global data-flow transformations;
- global loop and control-flow transformations;
- data reuse decision;
- ordering and bandwidth optimization;
- memory allocation and assignment;
- in-place mapping.

The first three steps refer to architecture-independent optimizations; that is optimizations of the form of source-to-source code transformations. If these transformations are not applied, the resulting memory allocation is very likely far from optimal. The remaining stages consist of optimization techniques that address target memory architecture.

Memory partitioning has demonstrated very good potential for energy savings (in [MAC 05], a survey of effective memory partitioning approaches is presented). The basic idea of this method is to subdivide the address space into several smaller blocks and to map these blocks to different physical memory banks that can be independently enabled and disabled [FAR 95].

Incorporating *scratchpad memory* (SPM) [PAN 00, PAN 99] in the memory architecture is another very popular technique in memory management for reducing energy consumption. A scratchpad is a high-speed internal memory used for temporary storage of calculations, data and other work in progress. There are many works on this topic, for instance [CHO 09], [KAN 05], [ANG 05], [RAM 05], [PAN 97b], [PAN 97a] and [EGG 08]. An SPM is a high-speed internal memory that is used to hold small items of data for rapid retrieval. In fact, both the cache and SPM are usually used to store data, because accessing to the off-chip memory requires a relatively longer time [PAN 01a]. The memory is partitioned into data cache and SPM to exploit data reusability of multimedia applications [SIN 03].

Methods on using SPMs for data accesses are either static or dynamic. Static methods [BAN 02, VRE 03, AVI 02, STE 02] determine which memory objects (data or instructions) may be located in SPM at compilation time, and the decision is made during the execution of the program. Static approaches generally use greedy strategies to determine which variables to place in SPM, or formulate the problem as an ILP program or a knapsack problem to find an optimal allocation. Recently in [AOU 10a], [AOU 10b], [AOU 10e], [AOU 10d], [AOU 10c] and [IDO 10], operation research techniques (e.g. tabu search, and genetic and hybrid heuristic) have been proposed for this problem. Dynamic SPM allocation places data into the SPM, taking into account the latency variations across the different SPM lines [CHO 09, VER 04, ISS 07, FRA 04].

In *memory allocation for high-level synthesis*, the application addressed involves a relatively small number of signals[4]. Thus, techniques for dealing with the memory allocation are scalar oriented and use a scheduling phase ([SCH 92, STO 92, BAL 07]). Therefore, the major goal is typically to minimize the number of registers for storing scalars. This optimization problem is called *register allocation* [GAJ 92].

ILP formulations [SCH 92, BAL 88], line packing [KUR 87, HUA 09], graph coloring [STO 92] and clique partitioning techniques [TSE 86] have been proposed for register allocation. One of the first techniques, a graph coloring-based heuristic, is reported in [CHA 04].

---

4 In literature, the term "signal" is often used to indicate an array as well.

It is based upon the fact that minimizing the number of registers is equivalent to the graph coloring problem. A graph is constructed for illustrating this problem. Vertices represent variables, edges indicate the interference (conflict) between variables and each color represents a different physical register. Many other variants of this coloring problem for register allocation have been proposed (e.g. see [BLA 10, ZEI 04, KOE 06]). More and more metaheuristic methods are used to find good solutions to this problem (e.g. see [SHE 07, TOP 07, MAH 09]). General approaches have been proposed for this problem (e.g. see [GRU 07, KOE 09, PER 08, PIN 93, CUT 08]).

We are only interested in the optimization techniques for memory architecture involving one-port memories. Consequently, the other techniques using multi-port or scratchpad are not addressed in this chapter.

1.3.3. *Data binding*

This section presents some references for the data binding problem, which is to allocate data structure from a given application to a given memory architecture. Because of the provided architecture, the constraints considered and the criterion to optimize, there is a wide range of data binding problems.

First, we introduce some interesting works about the memory partitioning problem for low energy. Next, we present the works that take into account the number and capacities of memory banks, and the number of accesses to variables. Finally, we discuss other works that consider the aforementioned constraints and use an external memory.

These works have similarities with the last three versions of the memory allocation problem addressed in Chapters 3, 4 and 5. A fixed number of memory banks is the main feature that they have in common. The two more complex versions of the memory allocation problem consider the memory bank capacities, the number of accesses to variables and the use of an external memory.

1.3.3.1. *Memory partitioning problem for low energy*

Section 1.3.1 introduced the memory partitioning problem, which is a typical performance-oriented solution, and energy may be reduced only for some specific access patterns. In contrast, the memory partitioning problem for low energy reduces the energy for accessing memories [BEN 02c]. The main characteristics of this problem are the fixed number of memory banks and the ability of independently accessing the memory banks.

There are some techniques to address the memory partitioning problem for low energy, and some different versions of this problem depending on the considered architecture.

In [KOR 04], a method for memory allocation and assignment is proposed using multi-way partitioning, but the partitioning algorithm to resolve the conflicts in the conflict graph is not described. In [KHA 09], a min-cut partitioning algorithm, initially proposed in [SHI 93], is used for memory allocation and assignment. To apply this algorithm, the conflict graph is needed and the designer must set a number of partitions (i.e. the number of memory banks). Moreover, the min-cut algorithm tends to find minimum cuts in the conflict graph, resolving minimum conflicts only. The conflict graph is modified so as to maximize the cuts. Maximizing the cut results in resolving the maximum number of conflicts in the conflict graph.

In [BEN 00b], Benini *et al.* propose a recursive algorithm for the automatic partitioning of on-chip memory into multiple banks that can be independently accessed. The partitioning is carried out according to the memory access profile of an embedded application, and the algorithm is constrained to the maximum number of banks.

In [CON 09], Cong *et al.* present a memory partitioning technique to improve throughput and reduce energy consumption for given throughput constraints and platform requirement. This technique uses a branch and bound algorithm to search for the best combination of partitions.

Sipkovà [SIP 03] addresses the problem of variable allocation to a dual memory bank, which is formulated as the max-cut problem on an interference graph. In an interference graph, each variable is represented by a vertex, an edge between two vertices indicates that they may be accessed in parallel, and that the corresponding variables should be stored in separate memory banks. Thus, the goal is to partition the interference graph into two sets in such a way that the potential parallelism is maximized, that is the sum of the weights of all edges that connect the two sets is maximal. Several approximating algorithms are proposed for this problem. Furthermore, [MUR 08] presents an integer linear program and a partitioning algorithm based on coloring techniques for the same problem.

1.3.3.2. *Constraints on memory bank capacities and number of accesses to variables*

The work presented in [SHY 07] takes into account memory bank capacities, sizes and the number of accesses to variables for addressing the problem of reducing the number of simultaneously active memory banks, so that the other memory banks that are inactive can be put to low-power modes to reduce energy consumption. The considered architecture has multiple memory banks and various low-power operating modes for each of these banks.

This problem is modeled like a multi-way graph partitioning problem, and well-known heuristics are used to address it [SHY 07].

A recent work that also considers the capacity constraints, sizes and the number of accesses is presented in [ZHA 11]. This paper proposes an ILP model to optimize the performance and energy consumption of multi-module memories by solving variable assignment, instruction scheduling and operating mode setting problems simultaneously. Thus, this model simultaneously addresses two problems: instruction scheduling and variable assignment. Two methods are presented for solving the proposed ILP model. The first method is a linear programming (LP)-relaxation to reduce the solution time, but it gives only lower bounds to the problem. The second method is a variable neighborhood search (VNS), which drastically reduces the computation time without sacrificing much to the solution quality.

Some heuristics to solve a buffer allocation problem applicable to explicitly parallel architectures are proposed in [MAR 03]. This problem is related to the multi-way constrained partitioning problem. Here, each partition is a set of buffers accessed in parallel and the number of buffers in each partition is less than or equal to the number of memory banks. The list of partitions is periodically executed. A set of memory banks of a fixed capacity is given. Thus, the objective is to compute an assignment of each buffer to a memory bank so as to minimize memory bank transfer overheads. All buffers have to be assigned and the buffers in the same partition are assigned to distinct memory banks.

1.3.3.3. *Using external memory*

In most cases, a processor requires one or more large external memories to store the long-term data (mostly of the DRAM type). In the past, the presence of these external memories in the architecture increased the total system power requirements. However, now these memories improve the throughput, but they do not improve the latency [NAC 01]. Some works that use an external memory are presented below.

Kumar, *et al*. [KUM 07] present a memory architecture exploration framework that integrates memory customization, which is logical to physical memory mapping and data layout. For memory architecture exploration, a genetic algorithm approach is used, and for the data layout problem, a heuristic method is proposed. This heuristic is used to solve the data allocation problem for all memory architectures considered in the exploration phase, which could be in several thousands. Hence, the heuristic must consider each architecture (on-chip memory size, the number and size of each memory bank, the number of memory ports per bank, the types of memory, scratchpad, RAM or cache) to perform the data allocation.

This heuristic starts considering the critical data (i.e. the data that have high access frequency) for designing an initial solution. Then, it backtracks to find changes in the allocation of data, which can improve the solution. These changes are performed considering the data size, and the minimum allocation cost of data in the memory bank.

Hence, the first step to build the initial solution is to identify and place all the critical data in the internal memory and the remaining data in the external memory. In the second step, the algorithm tries to resolve as many conflicts as possible (self-conflicts and parallel-conflicts) by using the different dual/single access memory banks. The data that are on self-conflict are first allocated and then the data on critical parallel-conflict. The metaheuristic first uses the dual-access memory bank to allocate data; the single-access memory banks are used only when the all dual-access memory banks are full.

Corvino *et al.* [COR 10] present a method to map data parallel applications into a specific hardware accelerator. Data parallel applications are executed in a synchronous architectural model. Initially, the data to be processed are stored in the external memory, and during the cycles of application, the manipulated data can be stored in local memories.

The general idea of the proposed method is to mask the times to transfer data with the time to perform computations. A method based on an integer partition is used to reduce the exploration space.

Most of the works presented in this section do not provide a mathematical model and a comparison with an exact method. Moreover, their proposed approaches are only tested on a single instance. In this work, we propose a formal mathematical model for each version of the memory allocation problem. Additionally, the proposed metaheuristics are compared with exact approaches on a large set of instances.

No version of memory allocation problem is totally concerned with the architecture, constraints and/or the criterion to optimize the problems presented in this section.

1.4. Operations research and electronics

This section is inspired from the works of the CNRS GDR-RO working group "Problématiques d'optimisation discrete en micro-électronique" [MAR 10a, MAR 10b, KIE 11].

In the last decades, researchers and practitioners of electronics have revealed needs for further optimizations. Additionally, even "old" problems have become more challenging due to the larger instances and increasing complexity of the architecture.

However, the complexity, size and novelty of problems encountered in microelectronics make this area a source of exciting and original optimization problems for the community of operations research (OR). Indeed, the models and data are complex and poorly formalized, and problems are often very challenging. Furthermore, the integration of more components on the circuit reveals new and/or large-size problems to model and solve.

These are the reasons why a new discipline has appeared at the border of operations research and electronics. This discipline is concerned with addressing electronic problems using operations research methods. Isolated experiments have first been reported, which explain both the heterogeneity in the electronic topics addressed, and the great diversity in the operations research methods used to solve them. The following paragraphs mention some examples of OR methods used for addressing electronics problems.

The development of modern algorithms for the placement problem is one of the oldest applications of OR to microelectronics. This problem consists of placing the elements of a circuit in the target area so that no elements overlap with each other, and the total length of interconnections is minimized. The circuits may have billions of transistors, and five times more connections. A team in Bonn, led by Bernhard Korte and Jens Vygen, work on this problem in collaboration with IBM. They develop combinatorial optimization methods [KOR 08], which are implemented in their solver called "Bonn Tools" [BRE 08]. Futhermore, [CHA 09] summarizes the algorithms implemented for this problem, which are mainly based on simulated annealing, min-cut and analytical placement basics.

Another well-known example of OR for electronics is the implementation of metaheuristics for the register allocation problem [SHE 07, TOP 07, MAH 09, BLA 10, ZEI 04, KOE 06, GRU 07, PER 08]), as mentioned in section 1.3.2.

Advanced metaheuristics have been designed for high-level synthesis tools [TRA 10, COU 09, TRA 08, SEV 11, ROS 08]. They are considered to be efficient approaches, and some of them have been implemented in the high-level synthesis platform, [GAU 93].

Many metaheuristics have been developed for the management of scratchpad memories ([AOU 10a, AOU 10b, AOU 10e, AOU 10d, AOU 10c, IDO 10]), and management of system on-chip ([DAF 08, CRÉ 10, KOR 04, DU 08]), as mentioned in section 1.3.2.

Some OR methods have been applied for evaluating communication processors [SEN 09], for very large scale integration (VLSI) [PEY 09], for improving the performance of ASICs chips [HEL 03] and for the memory architecture exploration [KUM 07, ZHA 11].

1.4.1. *Main challenges in applying operations research to electronics*

There is not a single scientific object of interest in the activity of operations research for electronics, and the operational researcher usually faces the following issues when entering the electronics field.

– The first difficulty is with *communication*. Generally, electronic practitioners do not have good knowledge of OR and vice versa. Often electronic designers are not interested in trying different methods that come from an unknown field of science, because they rely on their experience and competences to tackle the problems in their own field. Hence, at the beginning of a research project, electronic practitioners can be reluctant to work with an OR team and to communicate the electronic problems and needs.

– The microelectronic culture is difficult to access because of the large amount electronic subjects involved with microelectronics and a hermetic language employed by electronic practitioners. This language is related to technology and only numerous interactions make it possible to understand some terms.

Similarly, for electronic practitioners, entering into the OR field requires an adaptation time. Hence, the electronic practitioners, who design the conception tools, often develop their own heuristics, which are often considered poor by OR standards.

– The *objectives* of electronic industries and researchers are very different. The complexity of problems, the variety of techniques and time constraints presented in the industry suggest a "greedy" approach, which does not always make it possible to understand the nature of theoretical issues. Furthermore, the notion of the problem in the academic sense is often not known by the practitioners in the industry. Moreover, the choice of the optimization methodologies may be influenced by the application domain depending on whether or not the industrialists want to develop and partially or totally implement the proposed solutions (i.e. heuristics vs. algorithms). For these reasons, modeling the problem is crucial.

– Some *technological* difficulties may arise. The continuous development of miniaturized chips changes the properties of electronic components. All of this means that the operations research models are applied to problems whose dimensions are not necessarily known or even fixed. Thus, the problems can easily change over time. Hence, it is, here, more difficult to fix models than in other areas.

– Sometimes *data* are not easy to obtain. In the industry, information can be confidential or accessing it may take longer due to a large hierarchy in the administration. In some cases, there are no efficient tools to generate data. Also, for technological reasons in component design, the typical dimension of instances is often difficult to obtain.

– *Appreciation/Enhancement.*   Another   difficulty   is presented in the publication of results. Currently, there is no specialized journal dedicated to this kind of interdisciplinary work; and general OR or electronic journals do not easily accept these kinds of papers. In particular, electronic practitioners find it difficult to accept OR type communications in their journals and at their conferences. On the one hand, OR researchers are not familiar with the applications, motivations and vocabulary used in the electronic literature. On the other hand, it is not easy to explain and motivate the electronic problems in the OR community, and thus it is hard to capture the interest of an OR audience.

Chapter 2

Unconstrained Memory Allocation Problem

This chapter describes the first version of the memory allocation problem addressed in this book. This version is related to hardware optimization techniques discussed in Chapter 1 (see section 1.3.2). Hence, this version is focused on the memory architecture design of an embedded system.

In short, the unconstrained memory allocation problem is equivalent to finding the *chromatic number* of a *conflict graph*. In this graph, a vertex symbolizes a *data structure* (array) and an edge represents a *conflict* between two variables. A conflict arises when two data structures are required at the same time.

In this chapter, we do not seek a memory allocation of data structures but search for the minimum number of memory banks needed by a given application. Therefore, we do not search for a coloring, but we are interested in finding upper bounds on the chromatic number. We introduce three new upper bounds on the chromatic number, without making any assumption on the graph structure. The first one, ξ, is based on the number of edges and vertices, and is applied to any connected component of the graph, whereas ζ and η are based on the degree of the vertices in the graph. The computational complexity of the three-bound computation is assessed. Theoretical and computational comparisons are also made with five well-known bounds from the literature, which demonstrate the superiority of the new upper bounds.

2.1. Introduction

The electronic designers want a trade-off between the memory architecture cost, that is the size and number of memory banks, and the energy consumption. The power consumption is reduced as the size of a memory bank is decreased. The memory architecture is more expensive when the number of memory banks increases, because the addressing and control logic are duplicated, and communication resources required to transfer information increases [BEN 02c]. Therefore, in the design of memory architecture, it is extremely important to find the minimum number of memory banks required by an application. The minimum number of memory banks also helps us to define a reasonable size for them.

Thus, the purpose of this first version of the memory allocation problem is to provide a decision aid to the design of an embedded system for a specific application. Indeed, this problem is related to hardware optimization presented in section 1.3.2, and it shares common features with two problems discussed in the same section: the memory allocation and assignment problem and the register allocation problem. They both aim at finding the minimum number of memory banks/registers, and they also return the corresponding allocation of variables into memory banks/registers. The unconstrained memory allocation problem though only searches for the minimum number of memory banks needed in the target architecture of a given application.

The unconstrained memory allocation problem makes minimal hypotheses on the target architecture. The application to be implemented (e.g. Moving Picture Experts Group (MPEG) encoding, filtering or any other signal processing algorithm) is provided as a C source code. A *data structure* is defined as an array of scalars. We assume that the processor can access all its memory banks simultaneously. Then, when two data structures, namely a and b, are required at the same time for performing one or more operations of a given application, they can be loaded/stored (read/write) at the same time provided that a and b are allocated to two different memory banks. If they are allocated to the same memory bank, then they must be loaded/stored sequentially, and more time is needed to access data. Hence, a and b are said to be conflicting if they must be accessed in parallel to execute the instructions in the application.

A conflict is said to be *open* if its data structures are allocated to the same memory bank, otherwise it is said to be *closed*.

The data structures related to a conflict can be involved in the same operation, or they can be involved in different operations (see section 2.4 for examples). Moreover, an *auto-conflict* arises when a data structure is in conflict with itself. This case is present when two individual elements of the same data structure are required at the same time, for example a[i] = a[i+1].

Furthermore, data structures cannot be split and expanded over different memory banks. Also, it is possible that a data structure is not in conflict with any other data structure, that is the application could have isolated data structures.

The *access schedule* produced from C source file decides how data structures are accessed for performing the operations of a given application. It determines which data structures are accessed at the same time (in parallel), that is which data structures are in conflict. The access schedule also determines the order in which data structures are accessed, that is the order how the conflicts appear.

In the electronic literature, techniques for profiling the source code of embedded applications aiming at the optimization of the access schedule exist. Section 1.3.1 mentions the most important techniques for optimizing the code and the schedule. The importance of an optimal schedule in the memory allocation must be stressed. However, it is out of the scope of this work.

The unconstrained memory allocation problem can be stated as follows: for a given application, we search for the minimum number of memory banks for which all non-auto-conflicts are closed. In fact, an auto-conflict is always open, then it is not possible to find a solution without open conflicts.

The rest of this chapter is organized as follows: section 2.2 presents a mathematical formulation to this version of the memory allocation problem. Section 2.3 describes that addressing this problem is equivalent to finding the chromatic number of a conflict graph. Section 2.4 presents an example of the unconstrained memory allocation problem. Section 2.5 introduces three new upper bounds on the chromatic number. Sections 2.6 and 2.7 assess the quality of three upper bounds and section 2.8 concludes this chapter.

2.2. An ILP formulation for the unconstrained memory allocation problem

The number of data structures is denoted by n. The number of conflicts is denoted by o and conflict k is modeled as the pair (k_1, k_2), where k_1 and k_2 are two conflicting data structures.

In this ILP formulation, we use the number of data structures as an upper bound on the number of memory banks.

The decision variables of the problem represent the allocation of data structures to memory banks. These variables are modeled as a binary matrix X, where:

$$x_{i,j} = \begin{cases} 1, \text{ if data structure } i \text{ is} \\ \quad \text{mapped to memory bank } j, \quad \forall i, j \in \{1, \dots, n\} \\ 0, \text{ otherwise} \end{cases} \quad [2.1]$$

The vector of real non-negative variables Z represents the memory bank that is actually used.

$$z_j = \begin{cases} 1, \text{ if at least one data structure} \\ \quad \text{is assigned to memory bank } j, \quad \forall j \in \{1, \dots, n\} \\ 0, \text{ otherwise} \end{cases} \quad [2.2]$$

The mixed integer program for that problem is the following:

$$\text{Minimize} \ \sum_{j=1}^{n} z_j \qquad\qquad [2.3]$$

$$\sum_{j=1}^{n} x_{i,j} = 1, \quad \forall i \in \{1, \dots, n\} \qquad\qquad [2.4]$$

$$x_{k_1,j} + x_{k_2,j} \le 1, \quad \forall k_1 \neq k_2, \ \forall j \in \{1, \dots, n\}, \forall k \in \{1, \dots, o\} \qquad [2.5]$$

$$x_{i,j} \le z_j, \quad \forall i, j \in \{1, \dots, n\} \qquad\qquad [2.6]$$

$$x_{i,j} \in \{0, 1\}, \quad \forall (i, j) \in \{1, \dots, n\}^2 \qquad\qquad [2.7]$$

$$z_j \ge 0, \quad \forall j \in \{1, \dots, n\} \qquad\qquad [2.8]$$

The cost function of the problem, equation [2.3], minimizes the number of memory banks used to store the data structures of the application.

Equation [2.4] enforces that each data structure is allocated to exactly one memory bank. Equation [2.5] is used for ensuring that two data structures involved in a conflict k are assigned to different memory banks, except for the case where a data structure is conflicting with itself. Equation [2.6] sets z_j to 1 if memory bank j is actually used. Finally, $x_{i,j}$ is set as a binary variable, for all (i, j) and z_j is non-negative for all j (explicit integrability enforcement is not required).

An optimal solution to the unconstrained memory allocation problem can be computed by using a solver such as GLPK [GNU 09] or Xpress-MP [FIC 09]. However, an optimal solution cannot be obtained in a reasonable amount of time (more than one h) for medium-size instances. Indeed, the following section describes that this problem is equivalent to finding the chromatic number of a conflict graph. As the chromatic number is $\mathcal{NP}$-hard, so is the unconstrained memory allocation problem.

2.3. Memory allocation and the chromatic number

The access schedule of a particular application can be represented as a *conflict graph*. Figure 2.2 illustrates the conflict graph of a piece of code.

The conflict graph $G = (X, U)$ for the unconstrained memory allocation problem is defined as follows: each vertex x in X models a data structure (array of scalars) and an edge $u \in U$ models a conflict between two data structures. There are no multiple edges, that is two different conflicts between two data structures. Each auto-conflict is represented by a *loop*. We have an *isolated vertex* auto-conflict for each data structure that is not in conflict with any other data structure.

We can formulate the unconstrained memory allocation problem using this conflict graph as follows: finding the minimum number of memory banks such that two adjacent vertices are not allocated to the same memory bank.

In order to state the vertex coloring problem for our conflict graph, loops (auto-conflicts) and isolated vertices are removed. In this way, we have an undirected and simple graph. The vertex coloring problem is to assign a color to every vertex in such a way that two adjacent vertices do not have the same color, while minimizing the total number of colors used.

The chromatic number of the conflict graph is the smallest number of colors needed to color it. Consequently, memory banks can be modeled as colors, and addressing the unconstrained memory allocation problem is equivalent to finding the chromatic number of the conflict graph.

In the electronic chip CAD, the unconstrained memory allocation problem is solved repeatedly. Therefore, it is important to quickly estimate the number of memory banks required by the application. For these reasons, we are interested in upper bounds on the chromatic number. Upper bounds are of particular interest for memory management and register allocation, because they enable us to reduce the search space for non-conflicting memory/register allocations.

In the following section, we introduce the main bounds on the chromatic number found in the literature.

2.3.1. *Bounds on the chromatic number*

We give some formal definitions about the vertex coloring problem and the chromatic number. Also, we introduce some notations.

Formally, a coloring of graph $G = (X, U)$ is a function $F: X \to \mathbb{N}^*$, where each vertex in X is allocated an integer value that is called a color. A proper coloring satisfies $F(u) \neq F(v)$ for all $(u, v) \in U$ [DIE 05, KLO 02]. A graph is said to be α-colorable if there exists a coloring that uses, at most, α different colors. In that case, all the vertices colored with the same color are said to be part of the same class.

The smallest number of colors involved in any proper coloring G is called the chromatic number, which is denoted by $\chi(G)$. The problem of finding $\chi(G)$, as well as a minimum coloring, is $\mathcal{NP}$-hard and is still the focus of an intense research effort [BUI 08, CAR 08, MEH 96, MÉN 08].

We recall some elementary results on the vertex coloring problem and chromatic number. A graph cannot be α-colorable if $\alpha < \chi(G)$. The chromatic number equals 1, if and only if G is a totally disconnected graph, it is equal to $|X|$ if G is complete, and for the graphs that are exactly bipartite (including trees and forests) the chromatic number is 2.

Regarding lower bounds, the chromatic number is greater than or equal to the clique number denoted by $\omega(G)$, which is the size of the largest clique in the graph, thus $\omega(G) \leq \chi(G)$. However, this bound is difficult to use in practice as finding the clique number is $\mathcal{NP}$-hard, and the Lovasz number is known to be a better lower bound for $\chi(G)$ as it is "sandwiched" between the clique number and the chromatic number [KNU 94]. Moreover, the Lovasz number can be calculated in polynomial time.

Let G be a non-directed, simple graph, where $n = |X|$ is the number of vertices and $m = |U|$ is the number of edges. The degree of vertex i is denoted by d_i for all $i \in \{1, \ldots, n\}$, and $\delta(G)$ is the highest degree in G. The following upper bounds on $\chi(G)$ can be found in the literature (e.g. in [LAC 03], there is a good summary about upper bounds):

$-\chi(G) \le d = \delta(G) + 1$ [DIE 05, GRA 11].

$-\chi(G) \le l = \left\lfloor \dfrac{1 + \sqrt{8m + 1}}{2} \right\rfloor$ [DIE 05, GRA 11].

$-\chi(G) \le M = \max\limits_{i \in X} \min \, (d_i + 1, i)$, provided that $d_1 \ge d_2 \ge \cdots \ge d_n$ [WEL 67].

$-\chi(G) \le s = \delta_2(G) + 1$, where $\delta_2(G)$ is the largest degree that a vertex v can have if v is adjacent to a vertex whose degree is at least as large as its own [STA 01].

$-\chi(G) \le q = \left\lceil \frac{r}{r+1}(\delta(G) + 1) \right\rceil$, where r is the maximum number of vertices of the same degree, each at least $(\delta(G) + 2)/2$ [STA 02].

There exists some upper bounds on the chromatic number for special classes of graphs:

$-\chi(G) \le \delta(G)$, for a connected simple graph that is neither complete nor has an odd cycle.

$-\chi(G) \le 4$, for any planar graph.

In section 2.5, three new upper bounds on the chromatic number are proposed. In sections 2.6 and 2.7, the quality of these new bounds is compared with the upper bounds mentioned in this section.

2.4. An illustrative example

For the sake of illustration of the unconstrained memory allocation problem, we present an instance based on the LMS (least mean square) dual-channel filter [BES 04], which is a well-known signal processing algorithm. This algorithm is written in C and is to be implemented on a TI-C6201 target.

Figure 2.1 shows the source code and access schedule of this LMS dual-channel filter. This schedule was generated by the compilation and code profiling tools of SoftExplorer [LAB 06], which is a software of the Lab-STICC laboratory [LAB 11].

The data structures are the arrays defined at line 10 of the C code and the constants (lines 4–8) and integer variables (line 12) are not considered for the memory allocation.

The access schedule presents the data structures in conflict. In the schedule, LD means load/read a data structure and ST means store/write in a data structure. In the sixth ordering, the processor must at the same time load data structure X1 and store in H11 the result of operation executed in line 22 of code source.

SoftExplorer separately compiles the code presented at each loop or condition instruction. The first four orderings correspond to the operations executed in for loops of the main for loop (lines 16, 19, 25 and 28).

In this example, most of the conflicts are presented in the data structures involved in the same operations. Only the fifth and eighth conflicts involve data structures used in different operations.

Moreover, the last two orderings are the auto-conflicts, it is due to the optimization rules presented in the compiler gcc used by SoftExplorer. In the main for loop, data structures X1 and X2 are present two times (see lines 22, 23, 31 and 32), so they are considered only the first time when they appear in the loop. Thus, X1 and X2 are ignored in lines 31 and 32, respectively, and data structures H21 and H22 are in conflict with themselves.

Figure 2.2 shows the conflict graph from the access schedule. Each data structure is represented by a vertex and each conflict in the schedule is represented by an edge. The auto-conflicts (loops in the graph) are represented with a

```
1  /* LMS dual-channel filter */
2  /* E.SENN */

3  /* definition of constants */
4  #define L 1024
5  #define mu11 0.2
6  #define mu12 0.2
7  #define mu21 0.2
8  #define mu22 0.2

9  /* global variables */
10 int X1[1024], X2[1024], H11[1024], H12[1024], H21[1024], H22[1024],
   y1[1024], y2[1024];

11 void main()
   {
12   int y11, y12, y21, y22, e1, e2;

13   for(int k=0;k<L-1;k++)
     {
14     int n = (k+L-1)%L;

15     y11=0;            /*------------ first channel ------------*/
16     for(int i=0;i<L-1;i++)
17       {  y11 = X1[(i+k)%L]*H11[(L-1+k-i)%L]+y11; } /* convolution */
18     y12=0;
19     for(int i=0;i<L-1;i++)
20       {  y12 = X2[(i+k)%L]*H12[(L-1+k-i)%L]+y12; }

21     e1 = y1[n]-y11-y12;  /* error */
22     H11[(n+1)%L] = H11[n]+mu11*X1[n]*e1; /* adaptation of filter */
23     H12[(n+1)%L] = H12[n]+mu12*X2[n]*e1;

24     y21=0;            /*------------ second channel ------------*/
25     for(int i=0;i<L-1;i++)
26       {  y21 = X1[(i+k)%L]*H21[(L-1+k-i)%L]+y21; }
27     y22=0;
28     for(int i=0;i<L-1;i++)
29       {  y22 = X2[(i+k)%L]*H22[(L-1+k-i)%L]+y22; }

30     e2 = y2[n]-y21-y22;
31     H21[(n+1)%L] = H21[n]+mu21*X1[n]*e2;
32     H22[(n+1)%L] = H22[n]+mu22*X2[n]*e2;
     }
   }
```

Access schedule	
Ordering	**Access**
1	LD X1 and LD H11
2	LD X2 and LD H12
3	LD X1 and LD H21
4	LD X2 and LD H22
5	LD y1 and LD H11
6	LD X1 and ST H11
7	LD H12 and LD X2
8	LD H12 and ST y2
9	LD H21 and ST H21
10	LD H22 and ST H22

Figure 2.1. *Code and access schedule of LMS dual-channel filter*

dotted line, because they will be removed to state the vertex graph coloring problem. In this example, there are no isolated vertices.

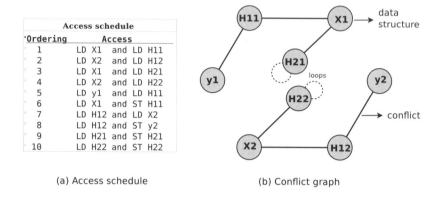

Access schedule	
·Ordering	Access
1	LD X1 and LD H11
2	LD X2 and LD H12
3	LD X1 and LD H21
4	LD X2 and LD H22
5	LD y1 and LD H11
6	LD X1 and ST H11
7	LD H12 and LD X2
8	LD H12 and ST y2
9	LD H21 and ST H21
10	LD H22 and ST H22

(a) Access schedule   (b) Conflict graph

Figure 2.2. *(a) Access schedule and (b) conflict graph of LMS dual-channel filter*

The chromatic number for the conflict graph without loops is two. Thus, it is necessary for two memory banks to find a memory allocation where all non-auto-conflicts are closed constraints.

2.5. Three new upper bounds on the chromatic number

The following lemma is required for proving Theorem 2.1, which introduces the first bound proposed.

LEMMA 2.1.– *The following inequality holds for any connected, simple graph $G_n = (V, E)$, where $m_n = |E|$.*

$$\frac{\chi(G_n)\,(\chi(G_n) - 1)}{2} + n - \chi(G_n) \leq m_n \qquad [2.9]$$

This inequality is referred to as equation [2.9].

PROOF.– Lemma 2.1 is proved by the recurrence on n.

First, it can be observed that Lemma 2.1 is obviously true for $n = 2$. Indeed, there exists a unique connected, simple graph on two vertices, it has a single edge, and $\chi(G_2) = 2$.

Second, we assume that Lemma 2.1 is valid for all graphs having at most n vertices. We now prove that the inequality of Lemma 2.1 holds for any connected, simple graph on $n + 1$ vertices. Let such a graph be denoted by G_{n+1}. It has m_{n+1} edges and its chromatic number is $\chi(G_{n+1})$.

G_{n+1} can be seen as a connected, simple graph G_n plus an additional vertex denoted by $n + 1$, and additional edges incident to this new vertex. The addition of vertex $n + 1$ to G_n leads either to $\chi(G_{n+1}) = \chi(G_n)$ or to $\chi(G_{n+1}) = \chi(G_n) + 1$. Indeed, the introduction of a new vertex (along with its incident edges) to a graph leads to increase in the chromatic number by at most one.

– First case: $\chi(G_{n+1}) = \chi(G_n)$
Adding 1 to equation [2.9] yields

$$\frac{\chi(G_{n+1})\,(\chi(G_{n+1}) - 1)}{2} + n + 1 - \chi(G_{n+1}) \leq 1 + m_n \leq m_{n+1}$$

We have $1 + m_n \leq m_{n+1}$ because at least one new edge is to be added to G_n for building G_{n+1}: vertex $n + 1$ has to be connected to at least one edge in G_n for G_{n+1} to be connected.

– Second case: $\chi(G_{n+1}) = \chi(G_n) + 1$
A minimum coloring of G_{n+1} can be obtained by keeping the minimum coloring of G_n, and by assigning color $\chi(G_{n+1}) = \chi(G_n) + 1$ to vertex $n + 1$. Since this coloring is minimum, there exists at least one edge between any pair of color classes [DIE 05]. In particular, this requirement for color $\chi(G_{n+1})$ implies that the degree of vertex $n + 1$ is at least $\chi(G_n)$, hence $m_n + \chi(G_n) \leq m_{n+1}$.

Adding $\chi(G_n)$ to equation [2.9] yields

$$\left(\frac{\chi(G_n)\,(\chi(G_n)-1)}{2}+\chi(G_n)\right)+n-\chi(G_n)\leq m_n+\chi(G_n)$$

The quantity in parenthesis is equal to the sum of the integers in $\{1,\ldots,\chi(G_n)\}$, and since $\chi(G_{n+1})=\chi(G_n)+1$,

$$\frac{\chi(G_{n+1})\,(\chi(G_{n+1})-1)}{2}+n-\chi(G_n)\leq m_n+\chi(G_n)$$

Finally, as $n-\chi(G_n)=n+1-\chi(G_{n+1})$ and $m_n+\chi(G_n)\leq m_{n+1}$,

$$\frac{\chi(G_{n+1})\,(\chi(G_{n+1})-1)}{2}+n+1-\chi(G_{n+1})\leq m_{n+1}$$

THEOREM 2.1.– *The following inequality holds for any connected, simple undirected graph G.*

$$\chi(G)\leq\xi,$$

with $\xi=\left\lfloor\dfrac{3+\sqrt{9+8(m-n)}}{2}\right\rfloor$

PROOF.– By Lemma 2.1, m can be lower bounded as follows:

$$\frac{\chi(G)(\chi(G)-1)}{2}+n-\chi(G)\leq m$$

This inequality leads to the following second-order polynomial in the variable $\chi(G)$:

$$\chi(G)^2-3\chi(G)-2(m-n)\leq 0$$

Once solved, this inequality leads to:

$$\chi(G)\leq\left\lfloor\frac{3+\sqrt{9+8(m-n)}}{2}\right\rfloor$$

Note that because all connected graphs have at least $n - 1$ edges, then $8(m - n) + 9 \geq 1$, thus the square root is in $\mathbb{R}^+$.

REMARK 2.1.– As this bound is only based on the number of the vertices and edges in the graph, it yields the same value for all graphs having the same number of vertices and edges. This bound computation requires $\mathcal{O}(1)$ operations.

THEOREM 2.2.– *For any simple, undirected graph* G, $\chi(G) \leq \zeta$, *where* ζ *is the greatest number of vertices with a degree greater than or equal to* $\zeta - 1$.

THEOREM 2.3.– *For any simple, undirected graph* G, $\chi(G) \leq \eta$, *where* η *is the greatest number of vertices with a degree greater than or equal to* η *that are adjacent to at least* $\eta - 1$ *vertices, each of them with a degree larger than or equal to* $\eta - 1$.

Before proving Theorems 2.2 and 2.3, some notations and definitions need to be stated. It should be noticed that connectivity is not required for the last two bounds, which involves more information on the graph topology than the first one.

The degree of saturation [BRÉ 79, KLO 02] of a vertex $v \in X$ denoted by $DS(v)$ is the number of different colors of the vertices adjacent to v. For a minimum coloring of graph G, $DS(v)$ is in $\{1, \ldots, \chi(G) - 1\}$ for all $v \in X$.

The following notations are used throughout this chapter:

$- C = \{1, \ldots, \chi(G)\}$ is the minimum set of colors used in any valid coloring.

– A valid (or proper) coloring using exactly $\chi(G)$ colors is said to be a minimum coloring.

– The neighborhood of vertex v denoted by $N(v)$ is the set of all vertices u such that edge (u, v) belongs to U. $N(v)$ is also called the set of adjacent vertices to v.

The last two bounds are based on the degree of saturation of a vertex and on Lemma 2.2.

LEMMA 2.2.– *Let F be a minimal coloring of G. For every color k in C, there exists at least one vertex v colored with k (i.e. $F(v) = k$), such that its degree of saturation is $\chi(G) - 1$ and where v is adjacent to at least $\chi(G) - 1$ vertices with a degree larger than or equal to $\chi(G) - 1$.*

PROOF OF LEMMA 2.2.– We prove the lemma by contradiction. First, we show that for all k in C, there exists a vertex v, colored with k, such that $DS(v) = \chi(G) - 1$. To do so, we assume that there exists a color k in C such that any vertex v colored with k has a degree of saturation that is strictly less than $\chi(G) - 1$.

Then, it can be deduced that for all $v \in X$ such that $F(v) = k$, there exists a color $c \in C \backslash \{k\}$ such that there does not exist $u \in N(v)/F(u) = c$. Consequently, a new valid coloring can be derived from the current one by setting $F(v) = c$. Indeed, v is not connected to any vertex colored with c. This operation can be performed for any vertex colored with k, leading to a valid coloring in which color k is never used. Hence, this new coloring involves $\chi(G) - 1$ colors, which is impossible by definition of the chromatic number.

Second, we show that, for every k in C, there exists a vertex v colored with k, whose degree of saturation is equal to $\chi(G) - 1$, and such that v has at least $\chi(G) - 1$ neighbors with degree larger than or equal to $\chi(G) - 1$. To do so, we assume that there exists a color k in C such that any vertex v colored with k having a degree of saturation equal to $\chi(G) - 1$ has strictly less than $\chi(G) - 1$ neighbors with a degree larger than or equal to $\chi(G) - 1$.

Then, it can be deduced that for every vertex v colored with k and such that $DS(v) = \chi(G) - 1$, there exists one color $c \in C/\{k\}$ such that the degree of any vertex $w \in V(v)/F(w) = c$ is strictly less than $\chi(G) - 1$. Then, for each vertex $w \in V(v)/F(w) = c$, there exists a color $l \in C\backslash\{k, c\}$ such that setting $F(w)$ to l yields a valid coloring. As a result, color c is no longer used in $N(v)$, thus $DS(v)$ is no longer $\chi(G) - 1$. This operation can be performed for any vertex v such that $F(v) = k/DS(v) = \chi(G) - 1$, leading to a coloring in which there is no vertex v colored with k and such that $DS(v) = \chi(G) - 1$. It can then be deduced from the first part of this proof that in such a situation, G can be colored with strictly less than $\chi(G)$ colors, which is impossible.

PROOF OF THEOREM 2.2.– It can be deduced from Lemma 2.2 that there exists at least $\chi(G)$ vertices in G, with a degree at least $\chi(G) - 1$. Thus, ζ being the greatest number of vertices with a degree greater than or equal to $\zeta - 1$, the following inequality holds: $\chi(G) \leq \zeta$.

REMARK 2.2.– It can easily be seen that Algorithm 1 which returns ζ, has a computational complexity of $\mathcal{O}\left(\max\{m, n\log_2(n)\}\right)$, as it requires enumerating the m edges to compute the degree of the vertices, $n\log_2(n)$ operations to sort the vertices and $\zeta \leq n$ iterations in the `while` loop.

Data: Graph $G(X, U)$; where $n \leftarrow |X|$ and $m \leftarrow |U|$.
Compute the degree, d_i, of all vertices i in X;
Sort the vertices by non-increasing degree;
$\zeta \leftarrow 0$, $stable \leftarrow 0$ and $i \leftarrow 0$;
while $stable = 0$ **and** $i \leq n$ **do**
    if $d_i \geq \zeta$ **then**
        | $\zeta \leftarrow \zeta + 1$;
    else
        $stable \leftarrow 1$;
    end
    $i \leftarrow i + 1$;
end

Algorithm 1. *Computing ζ*

PROOF OF THEOREM 2.3.– It can be deduced from Lemma 2.1 that there exist at least $\chi(G)$ vertices in G, which are adjacent to $\chi(G) - 1$ vertices with degrees larger than $\chi(G) - 1$. Since η is the greatest number of vertices with a degree greater than or equal to η that are adjacent to at least $\eta - 1$ vertices, each of them with degree larger than or equal to $\eta - 1$, then $\chi(G) \leq \eta$.

REMARK 2.3.– The proposed algorithm for computing η relies on the neighboring density. The neighboring density of vertex i is denoted by ρ_i and is defined as follows: ρ_i is the largest integer such that vertex i is adjacent to at least ρ_i vertices. Each of the latter has a degree greater than or equal to ρ_i. Algorithm 2 computes the neighboring density of all vertices. Then, η is computed by executing Algorithm 1, where d_i is replaced with ρ_i for all $i \in X$ and where ζ is replaced with η. The computational complexity for determining the neighboring density of all vertices is $\mathcal{O}(m \log_2(m))$, as it requires m operations to compute the degree and $2m \log_2(2m)$ operations to sort $2m$ numbers (the sum of degree of all vertices is $2m$). Therefore, the computational complexity for computing η is $\mathcal{O}(\max\{m \log_2(m), n \log_2(n)\})$.

Data: Graph $G(X, U)$; where $n \leftarrow |X|$ and $m \leftarrow |U|$.
Compute the degree of all vertices in X;
for $i = 1$ **to** n **do**

    Create the array tab by sorting the degree of the d_i neighbors of vertex i in non-increasing order;
    $\rho_i \leftarrow 0$, $stable \leftarrow 0$ and $j \leftarrow 0$;
    while $stable = 0$ **and** $j \leq d_i$ **do**

        if tab[j] $> \rho_i$ **then**
            $\rho_i \leftarrow \rho_i + 1$;
        else
            $stable \leftarrow 1$;
        end
        $j \leftarrow j + 1$;
    end
end

Algorithm 2. *Computing the neighboring density of all vertices*

2.6. Theoretical quality assessment of three upper bounds

The three bounds introduced in this chapter are compared theoretically to the five upper bounds from the literature, which were mentioned in the introduction, namely d, l, M, s and q.

PROPOSITION 2.1.– *For any simple, undirected, connected graph*

$$\xi \leq l$$

PROOF.– The number of edges in any simple undirected graph is less than or equal to $n(n-1)/2$, thus:

$$2m \leq n^2 - n$$
$$8m + 1 \leq 4n^2 - 4n + 1$$
$$8m + 1 \leq (2n - 1)^2$$
$$\sqrt{8m + 1} \leq 2n - 1$$
$$1 - 2n \leq -\sqrt{8m + 1}$$
$$4 - 8n \leq -4\sqrt{8m + 1}$$

Then, $8m + 5$ is added to the last inequality

$$9 + 8(m - n) \leq (8m + 1) + 4 - 4\sqrt{8m + 1}$$
$$\sqrt{9 + 8(m - n)} \leq \sqrt{8m + 1} - 2$$
$$\frac{3 + \sqrt{9 + 8(m - n)}}{2} \leq \frac{1 + \sqrt{8m + 1}}{2}$$
$$\left\lfloor \frac{3 + \sqrt{9 + 8(m - n)}}{2} \right\rfloor \leq \left\lfloor \frac{1 + \sqrt{8m + 1}}{2} \right\rfloor$$
$$\xi \leq l$$

PROPOSITION 2.2.– *For any simple undirected graph*

$$\eta \leq \zeta$$

PROOF.– This is obvious as the definition of ζ and η can be seen as the statement of two maximization problems. Since the requirements (or constraints) on η are more stringent than the requirements on ζ, the inequality $\eta \leq \zeta$ holds.

PROPOSITION 2.3.– *For any simple undirected graph*

$$\zeta \leq d$$

PROOF.– Since $\delta(G)$ is the maximum degree in the graph, $d_v \leq \delta(G)$ for all $v \in X$. By definition of ζ, there exists at least one vertex w with a degree greater than or equal to $\zeta - 1$, then:

$$d_w \leq \delta(G)$$
$$\zeta - 1 \leq \delta(G)$$
$$\zeta \leq \delta(G) + 1$$
$$\zeta \leq d$$

PROPOSITION 2.4.– *For any simple undirected graph*

$$\zeta = M$$

PROOF.– First, it is recalled that by definition of ζ, there do not exist $\zeta + 1$ vertices with a degree larger than or equal to ζ (otherwise this would be conflicting with the definition of ζ).

It is assumed without loss of generality that the vertices are indexed by non-increasing degree: $d_1 \geq d_2 \geq \cdots \geq d_n$. Then, it can be deduced that the vertices whose index is in $\{\zeta+1, \ldots, n\}$ have a degree less than or equal to $\zeta - 1$.

The vertex set $X = \{1, \ldots, n\}$ is split into two subsets: $X = A \cup B$ with $A = \{1, \ldots, \zeta\}$ and $B = \{\zeta + 1, \ldots, n\}$. In other words, A is the set of the ζ vertices of highest degree and B is the set of the $n - \zeta$ vertices of lower degree.

For all i in X, we denote by m_i the minimum between $d_i + 1$ and i (i.e. this makes it possible to write $M = \max\limits_{i \in X} m_i$).

For all $i \in X$, i is either in A or in B:

– If $i \in A$, then vertex i is such that $d_i \geq \zeta - 1$, that is $d_i + 1 \geq \zeta$. Moreover, by definition of A, $i \leq \zeta$. Consequently,

$$m_i = i \leq \zeta \leq d_i + 1 \qquad \forall i \in A$$

In particular, for $i = \zeta$, $m_i = \zeta$, and by definition of M, $\zeta \leq M$.

– If $i \in B$, then vertex i is such that $d_i \leq \zeta - 1$, that is $d_i + 1 \leq \zeta$. Moreover, by definition of B, $i \geq \zeta$. Consequently:

$$m_i = d_i + 1 \leq \zeta \leq i \qquad \forall i \in B$$

Finally, the inequality $m_i \leq \zeta$ holds for all $i \in \{1, \ldots, n\}$ and by definition of M this leads to $M \leq \zeta$.

REMARK 2.4.– Computing M by using the formula $M = \max\limits_{i \in X} \min\,(d_i + 1, i)$ provided in [WEL 67] has a computational complexity of $\mathcal{O}\,(\max\{m, n \log_2 n\})$, as it requires computing the degree of the vertices and sorting them by non-increasing degree. Although ζ and M are defined differently, their computation requires the same order of arithmetical operations.

PROPOSITION 2.5.– *For any simple undirected graph*

$$\eta \leq s$$

PROOF.– By definition of $\delta_2(G)$, there do not exist two adjacent vertices i and j in X such that $d_i > \delta_2(G)$ and $d_j > \delta_2(G)$. Consequently, it is impossible to find a vertex adjacent to at least $\delta_2(G) + 1$ vertices whose degrees are at least $\delta_2(G) + 1$. This shows that $\eta - 1$ is less than or equal to $\delta_2(G)$, that is $\eta \leq s$.

PROPOSITION 2.6.– *For any simple undirected graph*

$$\zeta \leq q$$

PROOF.– We prove by contradiction that $\zeta \leq q$ by using Proposition 2.4.

$$\zeta = M = \max_{i \in X} \min(d_i + 1, i)$$

We denote by A and B the two subsets of X: $A = \{1, \ldots, \zeta\}$ and $B = \{\zeta + 1, \ldots, n\}$.

As shown in the proof of Proposition 2.4:

$$i \leq \zeta \leq d_i + 1 \quad \forall i \in A$$
$$d_i + 1 \leq \zeta \leq i \quad \quad \forall i \in B$$

We assume that $\zeta > q$.

First, it is recalled that Stacho has proved in [STA 02] that $d_q < q$, that is $d_q + 1 \leq q$. Then, $\zeta > q$ does not hold if $q \in A$.

Second, if q belongs to B, it must satisfy $\zeta \leq q$ that is conflicting with the hypothesis $\zeta > q$.

Consequently, this proves that $\zeta \leq q$.

2.7. Computational assessment of three upper bounds

The new bounds introduced in this chapter are compared to the five bounds of the literature on the DIMACS instances [DIM 11] for vertex coloring. The detailed results are shown in Table 2.1 for 136 instances. The first three columns of this table provide the instance source at DIMACS, its name, the number of vertices and the number of edges. The next eight columns show the upper bound on the number of colors provided by the five bounds of the literature and the three upper bounds introduced in this chapter. The last three rows of Table 2.1 show the average value of each bound on the DIMACS instances, the penultimate row provides the average deviation to η over all the other bounds (note that these figures are not computed on the average numbers of colors), and the last row is the total amount of CPU time (in seconds) required for computing each bound on an Intel® Xeon® processor system at 2.67 GHz and 8 Gbytes RAM. Algorithms have been implemented in C++ and compiled with gcc 4.11 on a Linux system.

Instances			Known upper bounds					New upper bounds		
Source	Name	n/m	d	l	M	s	q	ξ	ζ	η
MYC	myciel3	11/20	6	6	5	4	6	6	5	4
MYC	myciel4	23/71	12	12	7	7	12	11	7	6
CAR	2-Insert._3	37/72	10	12	5	5	6	10	5	5
CAR	1-FullIns_3	30/100	12	14	9	12	12	13	9	7
CAR	3-Insert._3	56/110	12	15	5	5	7	12	5	5
MIZ	mug88_1	88/146	5	17	5	5	6	12	5	4
MIZ	mug88_25	88/146	5	17	5	5	6	12	5	4
CAR	4-Insert._3	79/156	14	18	5	5	8	14	5	5
SGB	queen5_5	25/160	17	18	13	13	17	18	13	13
MIZ	mug100_25	100/166	5	18	5	5	6	13	5	4
MIZ	mug100_1	100/166	5	18	5	5	6	13	5	4
CAR	2-FullIns_3	52/201	16	20	12	16	16	18	12	8
MYC	r125.1	125/209	9	20	7	7	10	11	7	6
CAR	1-Insert._4	67/232	23	22	9	9	16	19	9	7
MYC	myciel5	47/236	24	22	13	13	22	21	13	9
SGB	jean	80/254	37	23	12	14	19	20	12	11
SGB	queen6_6	36/290	20	24	16	16	20	24	16	16

Table 2.1. *Upper bounds on the chromatic number*

Instances			Known upper bounds					New upper bounds		
Source	Name	n/m	d	l	M	s	q	ξ	ζ	η
SGB	huck	74/301	54	25	11	21	28	22	11	11
CAR	3-FullIns_3	80/346	20	26	14	20	20	24	14	10
SGB	miles250	128/387	17	28	13	15	16	23	13	10
SGB	david	87/406	83	29	16	31	42	26	16	12
SGB	queen7_7	49/476	25	31	21	19	25	30	21	19
SGB	anna	138/493	72	31	15	51	37	28	15	12
CAR	4-FullIns_3	114/541	24	33	16	24	24	30	16	12
CAR	2-Insert._4	149/541	38	33	9	11	20	29	9	9
CAR	1-FullIns_4	93/593	33	34	18	33	26	33	18	13
SGB	games120	120/638	14	36	13	14	15	33	13	11
SGB	queen8_8	64/728	28	38	24	22	28	37	24	22
DSJ	dsjc125.1	125/736	24	38	17	20	24	36	17	12
MYC	myciel6	95/755	48	39	21	25	44	37	21	14
CAR	5-FullIns_3	154/792	28	40	18	28	29	37	18	14
MYC	r250.1	250/867	14	42	13	13	15	36	13	10
CAR	3-Insert._4	281/1046	57	46	9	13	29	40	9	9
SGB	queen9_9	81/1056	33	46	27	25	33	45	27	25
SGB	miles500	128/1170	39	48	29	35	35	47	29	25
CAR	1-Insert._5	202/1227	68	50	17	24	46	46	17	13
SGB	queen8_12	96/1368	33	52	31	30	33	51	31	27
SGB	queen10_10	100/1470	36	54	32	28	36	53	32	28
CAR	2-FullIns_4	212/1621	56	57	24	56	51	54	24	16
SGB	homer	561/1628	100	57	25	56	51	47	25	18
CAR	4-Insert._4	475/1795	80	60	9	15	41	52	9	9
SGB	queen11_11	121/1980	41	63	35	31	41	62	35	31
SGB	miles750	128/2113	65	65	42	55	57	64	42	37
MYC	myciel7	191/2360	96	69	35	49	88	67	35	23
SGB	queen12_12	144/2596	44	72	38	34	44	71	38	34
SGB	miles1000	128/3216	87	80	57	82	74	80	57	49
DSJ	dsjc250.1	250/3218	39	80	33	35	39	78	33	25
CAR	1-FullIns_5	282/3247	96	81	36	96	73	78	36	23
SGB	queen13_13	169/3328	49	82	43	37	49	81	43	37
CAR	3-FullIns_4	405/3524	85	84	28	85	72	80	28	20
REG	zeroin_i3	206/3540	141	84	41	38	119	83	41	32
REG	zeroin_i2	211/3541	141	84	41	38	119	83	41	32
DSJ	dsjr500.1	500/3555	26	84	23	26	27	79	23	18
MYC	r125.5	125/3838	100	88	61	70	85	87	61	52
REG	mulsol_i2	188/3885	157	88	53	34	139	87	53	33
DSJ	dsjc125.5	125/3891	76	88	63	72	72	88	63	57
REG	mulsol_i3	184/3916	158	89	54	34	140	87	54	33
REG	mulsol_i1	197/3925	122	89	65	82	111	87	65	51
CAR	2-Insert._5	597/3936	150	89	20	39	76	83	20	17
REG	mulsol_i4	185/3946	159	89	54	34	140	88	54	33
REG	mulsol_i5	186/3973	160	89	55	34	141	88	55	33
REG	zeroin_i1	211/4100	112	91	54	95	104	89	54	51
HOS	ash331GPIA	662/4185	24	91	20	23	25	85	20	16
SGB	queen14_14	196/4186	52	92	46	40	52	90	46	40
SGB	queen15_15	225/5180	57	102	49	43	57	101	49	43

Table 2.1. *(continued) Upper bounds on the chromatic number*

	Instances		Known upper bounds					New upper bounds		
Source	Name	n/m	d	l	M	s	q	ξ	ζ	η
SGB	miles1500	128/5198	107	102	84	106	96	102	84	78
LEI	le450_5a	450/5714	43	107	34	35	44	104	34	25
LEI	le450_5b	450/5734	43	107	34	35	43	104	34	26
SGB	queen16_16	256/6320	60	112	54	46	60	111	54	46
CAR	1-Insert._6	607/6337	203	113	33	69	136	108	33	25
CAR	4-FullIns_4	690/6650	120	115	36	120	104	110	36	24
DSJ	dsjc125.9	125/6961	121	118	109	113	116	118	109	106
HOS	will199GPIA	701/7065	42	119	35	35	42	114	35	28
MYC	r125.1c	125/7501	125	122	116	116	123	122	116	116
HOS	ash608GPIA	1216/7844	21	125	20	20	22	116	20	16
LEI	le450_15a	450/8168	100	128	57	68	93	125	57	39
LEI	le450_15b	450/8169	95	128	56	72	88	125	56	39
LEI	le450_25a	450/8260	129	129	63	85	114	126	63	46
LEI	le450_25b	450/8263	112	129	60	80	99	126	60	43
REG	fpsol2i3	425/8688	347	132	53	68	299	130	53	35
REG	fpsol2i2	451/8691	347	132	53	68	299	129	53	35
CAR	3-Insert._5	1406/9695	282	139	25	58	142	130	25	17
LEI	le450_5d	450/9757	69	140	52	53	68	137	52	41
LEI	le450_5c	450/9803	67	140	52	55	67	138	52	41
CAR	5-FullIns_4	1085/11395	161	151	49	161	142	145	49	28
REG	fpsol2i1	496/11654	253	153	79	102	231	150	79	67
CAR	2-FullIns_5	852/12201	216	156	56	216	193	152	56	31
DSJ	dsjc500.1	500/12458	69	158	59	61	69	156	59	47
HOS	ash958GPIA	1916/12506	25	158	21	22	26	147	21	17
REG	inithx_i3	621/13969	543	167	52	235	476	164	52	38
REG	inithx_i2	645/13979	542	167	52	235	476	164	52	38
MYC	r1000.1	1000/14378	50	170	41	47	51	165	41	34
SCH	school1_nsh	352/14612	233	171	101	115	195	170	101	84
MYC	r250.5	250/14849	192	172	119	154	166	172	119	99
DSJ	dsjc250.5	250/15668	148	177	126	134	141	177	126	116
LEI	le450_15c	450/16680	140	183	93	129	133	181	93	70
LEI	le450_15d	450/16750	139	183	92	129	131	182	92	70
LEI	le450_25c	450/17343	180	186	101	128	163	185	101	76
LEI	le450_25d	450/17425	158	187	99	138	145	185	99	75
REG	inithx_i1	864/18707	503	193	74	239	441	190	74	57
SCH	school1	385/19095	283	195	117	172	213	194	117	98
CUL	flat300_20_0	300/21375	161	207	144	148	155	206	144	135
CUL	flat300_26_0	300/21633	159	208	146	152	154	208	146	136
CUL	flat300_28_0	300/21695	163	208	146	157	158	208	146	136
GOM	qg.order30	900/26100	59	228	59	59	60	226	59	59
DSJ	dsjc250.9	250/27897	235	236	219	224	228	236	219	214
MYC	r250.1c	250/30227	250	246	238	242	246	246	238	236
CAR	3-FullIns_5	2030/33751	410	260	79	410	343	253	79	40
KOS	wap05a	905/43081	229	294	147	200	213	291	147	106
KOS	wap06a	947/43571	231	295	147	200	211	293	147	105
DSJ	dsjc1000.1	1000/49629	128	315	112	112	127	313	112	93
DSJ	dsjr500.5	500/58862	389	343	234	282	347	343	234	197
GOM	qg.order40	1600/62400	79	353	79	79	80	350	79	79

Table 2.1. *(continued) Upper bounds on the chromatic number*

Instances			Known upper bounds					New upper bounds		
Source	Name	n/m	d	l	M	s	q	ξ	ζ	η
DSJ	dsjc500.5	500/62624	287	354	251	260	277	353	251	236
HOS	abb313GPIA	1557/65390	188	362	123	119	184	358	123	94
CAR	4-FullIns_5	4146/77305	696	393	96	696	598	384	96	48
KOS	wap07a	1809/103368	299	455	188	259	275	452	188	130
KOS	wap08a	1870/104176	309	456	189	272	293	453	189	129
KOS	wap01a	2368/110871	289	471	174	223	270	467	174	115
KOS	wap02a	2464/111742	295	473	175	222	280	469	175	116
DSJ	dsjc500.9	500/112437	472	474	443	450	461	474	443	437
DSJ	dsjr500.1c	500/121275	498	492	478	489	490	492	478	476
GOM	qg.order60	3600/212400	119	652	119	119	120	647	119	119
MYC	r1000.5	1000/238267	782	690	472	535	696	690	472	396
CUL	flat1000_50	1000/245000	521	700	492	503	511	700	492	474
CUL	flat1000_60	1000/245830	525	701	493	501	515	701	493	472
CUL	flat1000_76	1000/246708	533	702	494	501	523	702	494	474
DSJ	dsjc1000.5	1000/249826	552	707	501	518	538	706	501	475
KOS	wap03a	4730/286722	345	757	230	302	333	752	230	148
KOS	wap04a	5231/294902	352	768	238	307	341	762	238	149
LAT	latinsquare10	900/307350	684	784	684	684	685	784	684	684
DSJ	dsjc1000.9	1000/449449	925	948	888	912	910	948	888	877
MYC	r1000.1c	1000/485090	992	985	957	976	978	985	957	951
GOM	qg.order100	10000/990000	199	1,407	199	199	200	1,401	199	199
MYC	c2000.5	2000/999836	1,075	1,414	1,000	1,028	1,054	1,414	1,000	962
MYC	c4000.5	4000/4000268	2,124	2,829	2,002	2,019	2,093	2,828	2,002	1,942
Average number of colors			186.1	218.5	122.2	147.5	171.2	215.9	122.2	108.9
Average deviation to η (in %)			−46.1	−58.3	−18.4	−29.4	−42.8	−56.6	−18.4	0.0
Total time (seconds)			0.2	0.0	0.3	2.1	0.3	3.8	0.9	14.0

Table 2.1. *(continued) Upper bounds on the chromatic number*

Table 2.2 is presented to assess the practical strength of Propositions 2.1–2.6. As each proposition is of the form $a \leq b$ (except Proposition 2.4), the last column of Table 2.2 indicates by which amount bound a is better than bound b (the average improvement is defined as the average value of $(a - b)/b$ over all the instances, in percent). Naturally, this amount is 0% in the particular case of Proposition 2.4, as it is an equality. It can be seen that ξ does not provide a significant advantage over l in practice.

However, Propositions 2.2, 2.3, 2.5 and 2.6 are stronger as the improvement is larger than 18%. More specifically,

Propositions		Average improvement
Proposition 2.1	$\xi \le l$	−4.56%
Proposition 2.2	$\eta \le \zeta$	−18.36%
Proposition 2.3	$\zeta \le d$	−35.99%
Proposition 2.4	$\zeta = M$	0.00%
Proposition 2.5	$\eta \le s$	−29.39%
Proposition 2.6	$\zeta \le q$	−32.02%

Table 2.2. *Computational assessment of Propositions 2.1–2.6 based on Table 2.1*

the best bound proposed in this chapter outperforms the best upper bound of the literature by more than 18% on average. Proving that $M = \zeta$ is important for highlighting the reason for the practical superiority of η over M. Indeed, η is based on the same principle as ζ, it focuses on the degrees of saturation of vertices. The difference is that η goes one step further than ζ by considering the degree of saturation of the neighbors of each vertex (i.e. the so-called neighboring density). This additional requirement has a computational cost that is drastically larger than the one required by computing ζ, but it provides a significant improvement in terms of the upper bound quality.

2.8. Conclusion

In this chapter, we have presented the first version of the memory allocation problem. This problem is equivalent to finding the chromatic number of the application's conflict graph. Three new upper bounds on the chromatic number have been introduced. The proposed upper bounds do not make any assumptions on the graph structure, they are based on basic graph characteristics such as the number of vertices, edges and vertex degrees.

The first upper bound, ξ, is based on the number of edges and vertices and only requires connectivity, whereas the last bounds, ζ and η, are based on the degree of the vertices in the graph.

We have theoretically and computationally assessed our upper bounds with the bounds of the literature. It has been shown that ζ is equal to an existing bound, while being computed in a very different way. Moreover, a series of inequalities has been proved, showing that these new bounds outperform five of the most well-known upper bounds from the literature. Computational experiments also have shown that the best bound proposed, η, is significantly better than the five bounds of the literature, and highlight the benefit of using the degree of saturation and its refined version (the neighboring density) for producing competitive upper bounds for vertex coloring. Indeed, using more information on graph topology appears to be a promising direction for future work.

The upper bounds on the chromatic number introduced in this chapter appear to be both significantly better than the literature bounds, and easily computable even for large graphs. However, there exist sophisticated metaheuristics for the vertex coloring problem (see e.g. [XIK 07, POR 10, HER 08, COJ 06, GON 02]), and advanced bounds (see e.g. [BUI 08, CAR 08, MEH 96, MÉN 08]) that reach better results than ours. But the computational time for getting these results and the associated coloring is sometimes longer than 20 minutes, which is far too long for the CAD electronic chip design in which the problem is solved. Indeed, memory allocation is only one part of the electronic chip design process, which is split in a series of sequential steps. Furthermore, as many design variations may be considered, the memory allocation problem has to be solved repeatedly, and CAD softwares are expected to be reactive enough to allow for "what if" studies. In conclusion, our bounds provide useful information for electronic designers. If the number of memory banks is greater than the minimum over ξ, ζ and η, then electronic designers are guaranteed to find a memory allocation where all non-auto-conflicts are closed.

The first two upper bounds were presented at the 2009 Cologne-Twente Workshop on Graphs and Combinatorial Optimization (see [SOT 09]), and a paper introducing the three new upper bounds by *Discrete Applied Mathematics* was published in 2011 [SOT 11b].

Chapter 3

Memory Allocation Problem With Constraint on the Number of Memory Banks

This chapter deals with the second version of the memory allocation problem addressed in this book. This problem is related to the data binding problems introduced in section 1.3.3. Hence, the aim of this problem is to allocate the data structures from a given application to a given memory architecture. The main characteristic in the memory architecture is that the number of memory banks is fixed.

The memory allocation problem with constraint on the number of memory banks is equivalent to *the k-weighted graph coloring problem* [CAR 66]. To address this problem, we propose an ILP formulation and two metaheuristics based on both the tabu search method and an evolutionary algorithm that have originally been proposed for the vertex coloring problem. The proposed approaches are tested on a set of instances. The results produced by these metaheuristics are encouraging, and they suggest that the adaptation of methods from graph coloring is a promising way to address memory allocation problems in embedded systems.

3.1. Introduction

In this chapter, we introduce the memory allocation problem with constraint on the number of memory banks. This problem is related to data binding problems presented in the optimization techniques for memory management and data assignment in section 1.3. Unlike the previous problem, which is focused on the design of memory architecture, in this problem the memory architecture is fixed. The purpose is to allocate data structures from a given application to memory banks of a given memory architecture.

In this version of the memory allocation problem, as in the memory partition problem for energy consumption (see section 1.3.3), the number of memory banks in the architecture is fixed. However, because of both different constraints considered and different objective functions to optimize, this version of the memory allocation problem is not equivalent to any problem related to the memory partition problem for energy consumption mentioned in section 1.3.3.

The number of available memory banks is limited because of cost and technological reasons. This is decided beforehand by the designer. Moreover, when the number of banks increases, both the communication resources required to transfer information and control logic increase at the same time. Hence, finding an optimal memory allocation for data structures with constraint on the maximum number of memory banks is extremely important [BEN 02c].

For this problem, we keep the assumptions on the target architecture from the previous chapter; that is the processor is able to simultaneously access all its memory banks, and the application to be implemented is provided as a C source code. Also, the data structures involved in the application have to be mapped into memory banks.

A conflict between two data structures is the same as it is defined in section 2.1. Moreover, we consider that each conflict has a *cost*, which is expressed in milliseconds (ms). This conflict cost is proportional to the number of times that the conflict appears in the application. Hence, the conflict's statuses, open and closed, are defined as follows:

– Closed conflict: two data structures are allocated to two different memory banks, as shown in Figure 3.1. The conflict does not generate any cost.

Memory banks

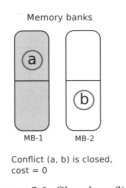

Conflict (a, b) is closed,
cost = 0

Figure 3.1. *Closed conflict*

– Open conflict: two data structures are mapped together in the same memory bank, as shown in Figure 3.2. The conflict generates a cost d_k.

In some cases, computing the conflict cost is not easy. Such a situation happens when the number of iterations of a loop cannot be forecasted (as in conditional instruction if or while loops). In this case, code profiling tools can be used for assessing conflict costs on a statistical basis [IVE 99, LEE 02].

Memory banks

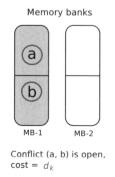

MB-1   MB-2

Conflict (a, b) is open,
cost = d_k

Figure 3.2. *Open conflict*

Figure 3.3 shows the access schedule and the cost conflicts for a piece of code. In this example, the probabilities of executing instructions if and else are 0.1 and 0.9, respectively. Data structures b and c are accessed in parallel two times in the schedule. Thus, the estimated conflict cost between data structures b and c is the number of iterations in the for loop multiplied by the probability of if instruction plus the product between the probability of else instruction and the number of iteration of its for loop, that is $10 \times 0.1 + 4 \times 0.9$ ms. For the conflict between e and f, it is 4×0.9. Consequently, forecasting the cost conflicts depends on the occurrence probability of conditional instructions.

```
if(p==0){              //( ----> 10%)
    for(i=0; i<10; i++)
        a[i] = b[i] + c[i];
    }
else{                  //( ----> 90%)
    for(i=0; i<4; i++)
    {   c[i] = e[i] + f[i];
        f[i]  = b[i];    }
    }
```

Access schedule	
Ordering	Access
1	LD b and LD c
2	ST a
3	LD e and LD f
4	ST c and LD b
5	ST f

Conflicts		Cost
b	c	4.6
e	f	3.6

(a) Piece of code   (b) Access schedule   (c) Cost conflicts

Figure 3.3. *Cost conflict*

This memory allocation problem, in addition to the fixed number of memory banks, takes into account the *conflict costs*. This problem, referred to as memory allocation with constraint on the number of memory banks, is stated as follows: for a given number of memory banks, we search for a memory allocation for data structures such that the total conflict cost generated by open conflicts is minimized. Section 3.3 presents an illustrative example that helps to understand this problem better.

The compiler often handles the allocation of data structures into memory banks; however, it does not produce optimal solutions. For this reason, section 3.2 presents an ILP formulation designed for this version of the memory allocation problem, and two metaheuristics are proposed in section 3.4, both are inspired by approaches designed to address the vertex graph coloring problem. The exact and heuristic approaches are compared in section 3.5.

3.2. An ILP formulation for the memory allocation problem with constraint on the number of memory banks

The number of data structures is denoted by n, the number of conflicts is denoted by o, and a conflict k is modeled as the couple (k_1, k_2), where k_1 and k_2 are two data structures.

This problem considers a fixed number of memory banks denoted by m, and the conflict costs associated with the conflicts, which are denoted by d_k for all $k \in \{1, \ldots, o\}$.

The particular cases of auto-conflicts and isolated data structures (discussed in section 2.2) are taken into account in this ILP formulation and in the metaheuristic approaches.

There are two sets of decision variables: the first set is defined by equation [2.1]; it is the binary matrix X, where $x_{i,j}$ is set to 1 if data structure i is allocated to memory bank j, for all i in $\{1, \ldots, n\}$ and for all j in $\{1, \ldots, m\}$ ($x_{i,j} = 0$, otherwise). The second set is a vector of real non-negative variables Y, which models the two conflict statuses, thus:

$$y_k = \begin{cases} 1, \text{ if the conflict } k \text{ is open} \\ 0, \text{ otherwise} \end{cases}, \quad \forall k \in \{1, \ldots, o\} \quad [3.1]$$

Thus, the integer linear program for this version of memory allocation problem is the following:

$$\text{Minimize} \sum_{k=1}^{o} y_k d_k \quad\quad\quad\quad [3.2]$$

$$\sum_{j=1}^{m} x_{i,j} = 1, \quad \forall i \in \{1, \ldots, n\} \quad\quad [3.3]$$

$$x_{k_1,j} + x_{k_2,j} \leq 1 + y_k, \quad \forall k \in \{1, \ldots, o\}, \forall j \in \{1, \ldots, m\} \quad [3.4]$$

$$x_{i,j} \in \{0,1\}, \quad \forall (i,j) \in \{1, \ldots, n\} \times \{1, \ldots, m\} \quad [3.5]$$

$$y_k \geq 0, \quad \forall k \in \{1, \ldots, o\} \quad\quad\quad [3.6]$$

Equation [3.2] is the cost function of a memory allocation of the data structures to memory banks. It is equal to the total sum of open conflict costs.

The following constraints guarantee a feasible solution: equation [3.3] is equivalent to equation [2.4]; both ensure that each data structure is assigned to a single memory bank. Equation [3.4] sets variable y_k to its appropriate value. Note that y_k is equal to 1 if conflict k involves a data structure in conflict with itself ($k_1 = k_2$). Equation [3.5] enforces integrability constraint on $x_{i,j}$. Finally, equation [3.6] sets y_j as a non-negative variable for all j.

We suppose that the required information to formulate this problem is supplied by the embedded system designer, more precisely by the code profiling tools applied to the C source code of the application.

The number of memory banks describes the architecture of the chip, and the number of data structures describes the application, whereas the conflicts and their costs carry information on both the architecture and the application.

This problem, without the auto-conflicts and loops, is equivalent to *the k-weighted graph coloring problem* [CAR 66, VRE 03] (this problem is also referred to as the *generalized graph coloring problem* in [KOL 95]). It consists of coloring the vertices of an undirected weighted graph with at most k colors so as to minimize the sum of the weighted edges having both their endpoints colored with the same color. In this problem, the vertices represent data structures and each edge represents a conflict between a pair of data structures.

The ILP formulation for memory allocation problem with capacity constraints on memory banks can be addressed using a solver like GLPK [GNU 09] or Xpress-MP [FIC 09]. However, as shown by the computational tests in section 3.5, an optimal solution cannot be obtained in a reasonable amount of time for medium-size instances.

Moreover, as the k-weighted graph coloring problem is $\mathcal{NP}$-hard [KAR 72, VRE 03], so is this version of memory allocation problem.

These are the reasons why we propose two metaheuristics to address this problem in section 3.4.

Vredeveld and Lenstra [VRE 03] tackle the k-weighted graph coloring problem using local search. In section 3.5, we compare the results reached by our metaheuristics, the ILP model and local search.

3.3. An illustrative example

We take up again the example of Chapter 2, with the aim of illustrating the memory allocation problem with the constraint on the number of memory banks.

In this example, the purpose is to allocate the data structures of the LMS dual-channel filter algorithm [BES 04] to the available memory banks.

SoftExplorer [LAB 06] produces the information required from the source code C (see Figure 2.1). To display data, SoftExplorer changes the name of data structures by numbers. For this application, we have H11= 1, H12= 2, H21= 3, H22= 4, X1= 5, X2= 6, y1= 7 and y2= 8.

There are two memory banks, and Table 3.1 presents conflicts and their costs produced by SoftExplorer.

Conflicts		Cost (ms)
1	5	1,047,552
2	6	1,047,552
3	5	1,046,529
4	6	1,046,529
1	7	1,023
2	8	1,023
3	3	1,023
4	4	1,023

Table 3.1. *Conflicts and costs of LMS dual-channel filter*

SoftExplorer computes the conflict cost using the access schedule. For example, conflict $(1, 5)$ represents the conflict between data structures H11 and X1. These data structures are accessed in parallel twice (ordering 1 and 6 in the schedule of Figure 2.2). Also, the first time this conflict appears (line 17 of Figure 2.1), it is in a double loop for. Thus, the conflict cost is $(L-1)^2 + (L-1)$, where $L-1 = 1,023$ (defined in line 4 of Figure 2.1) is the number of iterations in loops for.

A solution found by Xpress-MP is shown in Figure 3.4, where one can see the colored conflict graph and the allocation of data structures to two memory banks. The numbers on edges represent the conflict costs, and the loops are removed to state the k-weighted graph coloring problem.

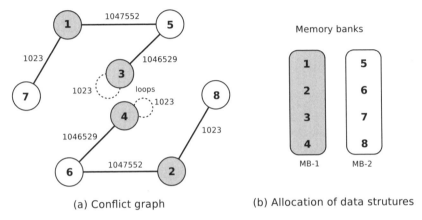

(a) Conflict graph   (b) Allocation of data strutures

Figure 3.4. *Optimal solution for the example for the memory allocation with constraint on the number of memory banks*

The chromatic number of this conflict graph is equal to the number of available memory banks thus all non-auto-conflicts are closed. The total cost of this memory allocation is the sum of the cost of the auto-conflicts; it is 2,046 ms.

3.4. Proposed metaheuristics

As the memory allocation problem with constraint on the number of memory banks is equivalent to a graph coloring problem (k-weighted graph coloring problem), we propose two metaheuristics based on coloring approaches. The first metaheuristic is inspired from *TabuCol*, which is a tabu search for the vertex coloring problem presented by Hertz and Werra [HER 87]. The second metaheuristic is a hybrid evolutionary algorithm based on *Evocol* (Evolutionary Hybrid Algorithm

for Graph Coloring), which is introduced by Porumbel *et al.*
[POR 09b]. These proposed metaheuristics are described in
more detail in the following sections.

3.4.1. *A tabu search procedure*

The first metaheuristic implemented for this problem is
called the Tabu-Allocation. It is based on the Tabucol
algorithm, which is a tabu search for a vertex coloring
problem.

The *tabu search method* [GLO 97] belongs to the local
search methods. It relies on a simple procedure: it iteratively
moves from the current solution to another solution in
its neighborhood [SÖR 03]. The neighborhood of a solution
depends on the characteristics of the addressed problem.
The local search procedures stop when a local optimum is
found. The tabu search escapes from the local optimum by
prohibiting to move from the current solution to a solution
presented in the *tabu list*, this is the origin of the method's
name. In general, the tabu list stores the last visited solution,
and it is updated in the First In First Out (FIFO) principle.

Tabu-Allocation is a tabu search method developed
here for the memory allocation problem with constraint on
the number of memory banks. The considered neighborhood
$\mathcal{N}(x)$ of a solution x is the set of solutions obtained from
x by changing the allocation of a single data structure. For
example, in a solution x, the data structure i is allocated to
the memory bank j, so a possible neighbor solution x' can be
obtained by moving i to another memory bank and keeping
the same allocation for the remaining data structures.

Thus, the tabu list contains the most recent moves of data
structures. These moves are denoted by the pair (i, j), which
means that data structure i cannot be mapped to memory

bank j. We denote by NT the size of the tabu list, that is the maximum number of prohibited moves.

The main characteristic of Tabu-Allocation is that the size of the tabu list is not constant. Every N iterations, Tabu-Allocation randomly changes the size of the tabu list. It uses the function $NT = a + N \times t$, where a is a fixed integer number and t is a random number between 0 and 2. This idea was inspired from Porumbel's work about the vertex coloring problem [POR 09b]. This is, also somehow, related to a reactive tabu search [BAT 94].

Algorithm 3 describes the general structure of Tabu-Allocation.

The data required by the algorithm are the number of data structures, the number of memory banks, the conflicts between data structures and their respective costs and the two algorithm's calibration parameters: the maximum number of iterations and the size of the tabu list. The algorithm returns the best memory allocation found for the data structures.

Tabu-Allocation starts with a random initial solution, that is data structures are randomly assigned to memory banks. Initial solutions generated in this way are feasible, because the capacity of memory banks is not taken into account in this version of memory allocation problem.

In the iterative phase, Algorithm 3 searches for the best solution in the neighborhood of the current solution during the maximum number of iterations, $Niter$. However, the research can stop before if a solution without open conflict is found because such a solution is optimal.

At each iteration, Tabu-Allocation seeks for the neighboring solution with minimum cost, no matter if it is worse than the current one.

Input: n data structures, m memory banks, conflict costs, $Niter$ number of iterations and NT size of the tabu list.

Output: [$Best$]: the best memory allocation found

Initialization:

Choose an initial solution s;

$Best \leftarrow s$;

$Iter = 0$;

Iterative phase

while (($Iter \leq Niter$) **or** ($cost(s) > 0$)) **do**
  //$cost(s)$: cost produced by the solution s
  Generate $s' \in \mathcal{N}(s)$, from s allocating data structure i to memory bank j such that $cost(s') < cost(s'')$, $\forall s'' \in N(s)$;
  if ((i, j) is not tabu) **then**
    $s \leftarrow s'$;
    Update the tabu list;
    if $cost(s) < cost(Best)$ **then**
      $Best \leftarrow s$;
    end
  end
  Compute the size of tabu list NT;
  $Iter \leftarrow Iter + 1$.
end

Algorithm 3. Tabu-Allocation

To escape from local optima and to explore other regions of the search space, the method does not permit us to allocate a data structure i to its past memory bank j for NT iterations, that is: a new solution is accepted if the pair (i, j) is not in the tabu list.

The tabu list is updated on the FIFO principle whenever the current solution changes. The best solution $Best$ is updated if the cost produced by the current solution is less than the cost of the best solution found so far.

3.4.2. *A memetic algorithm*

The second metaheuristic implemented for this problem is called `Evo-Allocation`. It is inspired by an evolutionary hybrid algorithm for the vertex coloring problem.

`Evo-Allocation` keeps the following characteristics from Evocol [POR 09b]: a multiparent crossover, the general way of crossing parents and the variable size of tabu list. In fact, `Evo-Allocation` recourses to `Tabu-Allocation` for improving offspring.

The main difference between `Evo-Allocation` and Evocol is the way of updating population. `Evo-Allocation` considers the variance of the costs in the population to control diversity in the population.

`Evo-Allocation` is shown in Algorithm 4.

To execute the algorithm, the number of data structures, the number of memory banks and the two algorithms' parameters, r, number of parents for the crossover and g, number of offsprings produced at each iteration, are required. The algorithm returns the best solution found.

The algorithm starts generating an initial population at random. The general principle of `Evo-Allocation` is to obtain g new offsprings (new solution) by crossing r different parents (i.e. r elements of the current population). The crossover selects, in each parent, the best assignments of data structures to form an offspring. Each offspring produced by this way is improved using `Tabu-Allocation`.

Input: n data structures, m number of memory bank,
conflict and cost conflicts, number of parents r
involved and the number of offspring g produced
at each iteration.
Output: *Best* : the best solution found.
`Initialization`
Generate a random population of d elements;
`Iterative phase`
while *the stopping criterion is not satisfied* **do**
  while *g offspring are not produced* **do**
    Choose r parents ($r > 2$);
    Cross parents to produce a new offspring s;
    Apply `Tabu-Allocation` to new offspring s;
    Accept or not the offspring s;
  end
  Update population with g offspring, and update *Best*.
end

Algorithm 4. `Evo-Allocation`

Algorithm 5 describes the multiparent crossover. For each memory bank, the crossover chooses the allocations of data structures that minimizes the *conflict rate*. The conflict rate of a memory bank is the number of conflicts between its data structures, divided by the number of data structures mapped to this memory bank. The selected affectations are removed from each parent. Finally, to assign the remaining data structure, the algorithm chooses the memory bank that produces the minimum number of open conflicts.

`Evo-Allocation` produces an offspring if the *distance* to its parents is greater than a fixed threshold. The distance between two solutions s_a and s_b is defined as the minimum number of data structures that need to be moved from the first solution to become equal to the second solution. This definition is frequently used in graph coloring [GAL 99].

Input: r parents.
Output: an offspring.
for $j = 1, \ldots, m$ **do**

> **for** *each parent in* $1, \ldots, r$ **do**
> > | Compute the conflict rate of memory bank j
>
> **end**
> Choose the parent with minimum conflict rate
> Allocate its data structures to memory bank j to build
> the offspring
> **for** *Each parent in* $1, \ldots, r$ **do**
> > | Remove the data structures assigned to offspring
>
> **end**

end
Assign the remaining data structures to minimize the
total cost.

Algorithm 5. `Crossover-Evo-Allocation`

At each iteration, `Evo-Allocation` improves the quality of the population by replacing the g parents that have the highest cost with g offspring.

With the aim of ensuring diversity, `Evo-Allocation` considers the statistic variance of solution costs. If this variance is less than the fixed threshold, then a new population is randomly generated.

Thus, the population is updated with the offspring and with the variance criterion. This way of updating the population is a trade-off between diversity and quality.

3.5. Computational results and discussion

This section presents the instances used for the computational test, and the relevant aspects about the implementation of the proposed metaheuristics. Moreover, we present the results produced by our algorithms, and we compare these results with results of the ILP model and the local search method.

3.5.1. *Instances*

We have used 17 instances to test our approaches. The instance mpeg2enc is a real electronic problem provided by the Lab-STICC laboratory. No more real-life instances are available for this problem, so we have tested our algorithms using a set of instances that originates from DIMACS [POR 09a], a well-known collection of graph coloring instances. These instances have been enriched by generating edge costs at random so as to create conflict costs. For this, we have used the uniform law in the interval $[1; 100]$.

3.5.2. *Implementation*

Our metaheuristics have been implemented in C++ and compiled with gcc 4.11. The PC used is a 3 GHz Intel® Pentium IV with and 1 GB of RAM.

To execute Tabu-Allocation, we set the number of iterations $Niter$ equal to 10,000, and the integer numbers a and N used in function to calculate the size of the tabu list ($NT = a + N \times t$) are set to 50 and 10, respectively. We set these values based on our computational tests.

The calibration parameters of Evo-Allocation have the same value as in Evocol [POR 09b]: a population constituted of $d = 15$ elements, a crossover with three parents ($r = 3$) and the generation of three offspring ($g = 3$). The Tabu-Allocation embedded in Evo-Allocation is run with $Niter$ equal to 1,000.

The acceptance threshold for the distance between two elements of the population is $R = 0, 1 \times n$. We have fixed a threshold of 0.3 for the variance of the population, and 100 iterations as the stopping criterion.

3.5.3. *Results*

To our best knowledge, there are no alternative approaches for this problem in the literature. The k-weighted graph coloring problem can be addressed by Local Search [VRE 03], so we have tested the local search on instances of this memory allocation problem. To this end, we have used LocalSolver 1.0 [INN 10], which is a solver for combinatorial optimization entirely based on local search. This solver addresses a combinatorial optimization problem by performing autonomous moves, which can be viewed as a structured ejection chains applied to the hypergraph induced by boolean variables and constraints [REG 04]. Results of that method are also reported.

Table 3.2 provides the best cost reached by the metaheuristics, the local search solved with LocalSolver and also by the ILP formulation solved by GLPK [GNU 09]. The CPU time, in seconds, is provided for each method. The first two columns are the main features of the instances: name, number of data structures, number of conflicts and number of memory banks. The instances are sorted in a non-decreasing order of the number of conflicts. The last column shows each instance, if the solution found by GLPK is optimal or not, as we have set a time limit of 1 h for each instance.

The last lines of Table 3.2 give a summary for each approach used in this experiment; it is the number of optimal solutions, the number of best solutions and the average CPU time.

Instances		Tabu-Allocation		Evo-Allocation		Local Solver		ILP		
Name	$n \backslash o \backslash m$	Cost	Time	Cost	Time	Cost	Time	Cost	Time	Optimal
myciel3	11 \20 \2	**146**	0.26	**146**	1.82	270	3,600	**146**	0.03	yes
myciel4	23 \71 \3	**69**	0.52	**69**	2.47	92	3,600	**69**	1.16	yes
mug88_1	88 \146 \2	**967**	1.09	**967**	15.72	1,570	3,600	**967**	157.23	yes
mug88_25	88 \146 \2	**881**	1.07	**881**	16.27	1,163	3,600	**881**	53.11	yes
queen5_5	25 \160 \3	**974**	0.73	**974**	3.68	1,085	3,600	**974**	492.38	yes
mug100_1	100 \166 \2	1,149	1.19	**1,129**	26.79	1,818	3,600	**1,129**	957.19	yes
mug100_25	100 \166 \2	**1,142**	1.24	**1,142**	18.54	1,598	3,600	**1,142**	562.00	yes
r125.1	125 \209 \3	346	1.22	346	28.87	456	3,600	425	3,599.73	no
mpeg2enc	180 \227 \2	**32.09**	1.60	**32.09**	3.20	38.3	3,600	**32.09**	107.79	yes
myciel5	47 \236 \3	591	0.81	591	3.60	910	3,600	591	3,599.41	no
queen6_6	36 \290 \4	999	1.13	999	5.73	1,133	3,600	1,253	3,599.29	no
queen7_7	49 \476 \4	1,896	1.46	1,896	16.10	2,405	3,600	2,430	3,600.02	no
queen8_8	64 \728 \5	1,617	2.06	1,617	54.12	2,206	3,600	2,443	3,600.01	no
myciel6	95 \755 \2	9,017	1.26	9,017	18.52	9,965	3,600	9,963	3,600.43	no
myciel7	191 \2,360 \4	2,262	2.21	2,262	55.93	3,297	3,600	4,642	3,607.71	no
r125.5	125 \3,838 \18	785	8.58	734	156.97	1,394	3,600	1,668	3,648.99	no
r125.1c	125 \7,501 \23	2,719	11.27	2,685	135.24	4,159	3,600	-	3,820.08	no
Number of optimal solutions		7		8		0		8		
Number of best solutions		7		9		0		1		
Average CPU time		2.22		33.15		3,600		2,059.21		

Table 3.2. *Results*

3.5.4. *Discussion*

The computational results show that `Evo-Allocation` reaches the optimal solution when it is known, that is when the ILP can be solved to optimality within one hour. Obviously, `Tabu-Allocation` is faster than `Evo-Allocation` because `Tabu-Allocation` is a subprogram of `Evo-Allocation`. The local search has not reached the optimal solution for any instance after one hour of computation.

When the optimal solution is not found after one hour of computation for the ILP, the solution returned is worse than the solutions generated by the metaheuristics. Also, note that GLPK has not found any integer solution for the instance `r125.1c` after one hour of computation.

3.6. Conclusion

In addition to the ILP formulation, this chapter has introduced two metaheuristics: `Evo-Allocation` based on an hybrid evolutionary algorithm and `Tabu-Allocation` based on the tabu search method. These metaheuristics are inspired by the algorithms for the vertex coloring problem because this version of memory allocation problem can be seen as the k-weighted graph coloring problem.

The best results are returned by `Evo-Allocation`, which has a rigorous control of population diversity and a multiparent crossover. The main difference between `Tabu-Allocation` and a classical tabu search is the variable size of the tabu list.

Table 3.2 compares the results between metaheuristics and exact formulation solved with Xpress-MP. The experimental results are encouraging and suggest that the solutions found are of very good quality, even for larger instances for which the optimal solution is unknown.

Finally, the results suggest that the methods from graph coloring can be successfully extended to more complex memory allocation problems in embedded systems, which is done in the rest of this book.

The work presented in this chapter has been published in the proceedings of ROADEF (*Congrès de la société Française de Recherche Opérationnelle et d'Aide à la Décision*) [SOT 10].

Chapter 4

General Memory Allocation Problem

This chapter addresses the third version of the memory allocation problem. This problem is related to the data binding problems described in the state of the art, section 1.3.3. The general objective is the allocation of the data structures from a specific application to a given memory architecture. Compared to the problem of the previous chapter, additional constraints on the memory banks and data structures are considered. Moreover, an external memory is now present in the target architecture.

The metaheuristics designed for the previous version of the memory allocation problem are no longer used for addressing the problem of this chapter, because they require too much CPU time to return good solutions. This chapter discusses an exact approach and a variable neighborhood search (VNS)-based metaheuristic to tackle the general memory allocation problem. Numerical experiments are conducted on a set of instances, and statistical analysis is used to assess the results. The proposed metaheuristic appears to be suitable for the electronic design needs of today and tomorrow.

4.1. Introduction

The general memory allocation problem, called *MemExplorer*, is discussed in this chapter. This problem is focused on the allocation of the data structures from a given application to a given memory architecture. MemExplorer is more realistic than the previous version of the memory allocation problem presented in Chapter 3. In addition to memory banks, an *external memory* is considered in the target architecture. External memories store the long-term data, and they improve the throughput of an embedded system [NAC 01].

In this problem, the number of memory banks is fixed and the memory bank capacities are limited. The sizes of data structures and the number of accesses to them are both taken into account. Moreover, the time for accessing to the external memory is also considered.

In the data binding problem presented in section 1.3.3, we have mentioned some works that consider the capacities of memory banks and the number of accesses to data structures, and other works that use an external memory bank in the target architecture. Although MemExplorer has some similarities with the data binding problems, it is not equivalent to any of them. This is mainly due to the fact that the architecture, the constraints and the objective function are all different.

Assumptions similar to those in the previous version of memory allocation are considered in this problem. It is assumed that the application to be implemented (e.g. MPEG encoding, filtering and other signal processing algorithms) is provided as a C source code, and the data structures involved have to be mapped into memory bank. And all memory banks can be accessed simultaneously.

Hence, a conflict between two data structures is defined as in Chapters 2 and 3, and the cost of conflicts is also taken into account. A conflict is open when its data structures are allocated to the same memory bank, so a cost is generated. A conflict is closed when the conflicting data structures are mapped in different memory banks, so no cost is generated.

Due to cost and technological reasons, the number and the capacity of memory banks are limited; an external memory with unlimited capacity is then assumed to be available for storing data (it models the mass memory storage).

The processor requires access to data structures in order to execute the operations (or instructions) of the application. The access time to data structure is expressed in milliseconds (ms), and depends on its current allocation. If a data structure is allocated to a memory bank, its total access time is equal to the number of times the processor accesses it, because the transfer rate from a memory bank to the processor is 1 ms. If a data structure is allocated to the external memory, its access time is equal to its number of accesses multiplied by p ms, because the transfer rate from the external memory to the processor is p ms.

Figure 4.1 shows the memory architecture considered for this problem.

A good management of memory allocation allows decreasing the energy consumption. In fact, electronic practitioners consider that to some extent, minimizing power consumption is equivalent to minimizing the running time of an application on a given architecture [CHI 02]. As a result, memory allocation must be such that the loading operations are performed in parallel as often as possible. With this aim, the general memory allocation problem is stated as follows: for a given number of capacitated memory banks and an external memory, we search for a memory allocation for data structures such that the time spent accessing these data is minimized. Section 4.3 presents an instance of MemExplorer aimed at exemplifying this problem.

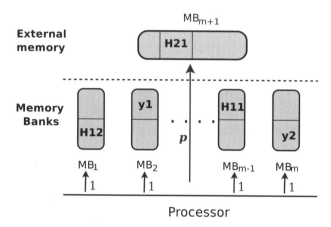

Figure 4.1. *The memory architecture for MemExplorer*

Electronics practitioners often left to the compiler the management of the data structures into memory banks. Nevertheless, the solution found by the compiler is often too far from the optimal memory allocation. In this work, we seek for better alternatives to manage the general memory allocation problem. Hence, an integer linear program is designed for MemExplorer in the following section. In section 4.4, we discuss metaheuristics conceived for this problem. The results produced by the exact method and heuristic approaches are presented, and statistically compared in section 4.5.

4.2. ILP formulation for the general memory allocation problem

The number of memory banks is denoted by m. Memory bank $m + 1$ refers to the external memory. The capacity of memory bank j is c_j for all $j \in \{1, \ldots, m\}$ (it is recalled that the external memory is not subject to capacity constraint).

The number of data structures is denoted by n. The size of a data structure i is denoted by s_i for all $i \in \{1, \ldots, n\}$. Besides its size, each data structure i is also characterized by the number of times that the processor accesses it, it is denoted by e_i for all $i \in \{1, \ldots, n\}$. e_i represents the time required to access data structure i if it is mapped to a memory bank. If a data structure i is mapped to the external memory its access time is equal to $p \times e_i$.

Conflict k is associated with its conflict cost d_k, for all $k \in \{1, \ldots, o\}$, where o is the number of conflicts.

Sizes and capacities are expressed in the same memory capacity unit, typically kilobytes (kB). Conflict costs and access time are expressed in the same time unit, typically milliseconds.

The isolated data structures, and the case where a data structure is conflicting with itself are both taken into account for the ILP formulation and for the proposed metaheuristics.

There are two sets of decision variables; the first set represents the allocation of data structures to memory banks. These variables are modeled as a binary matrix X, where:

$$x_{i,j} = \begin{cases} 1, \text{if data structure } i \text{ is mapped} \\ \quad \text{to memory bank } j \\ 0, \text{otherwise} \end{cases} , \quad \begin{cases} \forall i \in \{1, \ldots, n\}, \\ \forall j \in \{1, \ldots, m+1\} \end{cases} \text{[4.1]}$$

The second set is a vector of real non-negative variables Y, which models the conflict statuses; so variable y_k associated with conflict k has two possible values:

$$y_k = \begin{cases} 1, \text{if conflict } k \text{ is closed} \\ 0, \text{otherwise} \end{cases} , \quad \forall k \in \{1, \ldots, o\} \qquad \text{[4.2]}$$

The mixed integer program for the general memory allocation problem is as follows:

$$\text{Minimize } \sum_{i=1}^{n}\sum_{j=1}^{m} e_i x_{i,j} + p \sum_{i=1}^{n} e_i x_{i,m+1} - \sum_{k=1}^{o} y_k d_k \quad [4.3]$$

$$\sum_{j=1}^{m+1} x_{i,j} = 1, \qquad \forall i \in \{1,\ldots,n\} \qquad [4.4]$$

$$\sum_{i=1}^{n} x_{i,j} s_i \le c_j, \qquad \forall j \in \{1,\ldots,m\} \qquad [4.5]$$

$$x_{k_1,j} + x_{k_2,j} \le 2 - y_k, \quad \forall j \in \{1,\ldots,m+1\}, \quad \forall k \in \{1,\ldots,o\} \quad [4.6]$$

$$x_{i,j} \in \{0,1\}, \qquad \forall(i,j) \in \{1,\ldots,n\} \times \{1,\ldots,m\} \quad [4.7]$$

$$y_k \ge 0 \qquad \forall k \in \{1,\ldots,o\} \qquad [4.8]$$

The cost function of the problem, equation [4.3], is the total time spent accessing the data structures and storing them in the appropriate registers to perform the required operations listed in the C file. It is expressed in milliseconds.

This cost function is the sum of three terms. The first term is the cost generated by accessing to data structures into memory banks, whereas the second term is the cost produced by accessing to data structures placed in the external memory. The last term is the sum of the closed conflicts. Note that all conflict costs are involved in the sum of the first two terms. The last term is negative, and thus, only the open conflicts are presented in the objective function.

Because $\sum_{i=1}^{n}\sum_{j=1}^{m+1} e_i x_{i,j} = \sum_{i=1}^{n} e_i$ is a constant value, it is equivalent to minimize:

$$(p-1)\sum_{i=1}^{n}\left(e_i x_{i,m+1}\right) - \sum_{k=1}^{o} y_k d_k \qquad [4.9]$$

Equation [4.4] enforces that each data structure is allocated either to a unique memory bank or to the external memory. Equation [4.5] is used for ensuring that the total size of the data structures allocated to a memory bank does not exceed its capacity. For any conflict k, variable y_k must be set appropriately; this is enforced by equation [4.6]. For an auto-conflict k, y_k is equal to 1. Finally, $x_{i,j}$ is a binary variable, for all (i, j), and y_k is non-negative for all k.

The number of memory banks with their capacities, the external memory and transfer rate p ms describe the architecture of the chip. The number of data structures, their size and access time describe the application, whereas the conflicts and their costs carry information about both the architecture and the application.

Note that this problem is similar to the *k-weighted graph coloring problem* [CAR 66] if memory banks are not subject to capacity constraints, or if their capacity is large enough for holding all the data structures. In fact, in that case the external memory is no longer used and the size, as well as the access cost of data structures, can be ignored.

An optimal solution to MemExplorer problem can be computed by using a solver such as GLPK [GNU 09] or Xpress-MP [FIC 09]. However, as shown by the computational tests in section 4.5, an optimal solution cannot be obtained in a reasonable amount of time for medium-size instances. Moreover, MemExplorer is $\mathcal{NP}$-hard, because it generalizes the k-weighted graph coloring problem [CAR 66].

In the following section, we propose a VNS-based metaheuristic for addressing this problem. Vredeveld and Lenstra [VRE 03] address the k-weighted graph coloring problem by local search programming. We compare the results reached by ILP formulation, our metaheuristic approaches and local search programming in section 4.5. Moreover, we use a statistical test to analyze the performance of these approaches.

4.3. An illustrative example

This is an instance produced from a least mean square (LMS) dual-channel filter [BES 04]. It exemplifies the general memory allocation problem. The information yield from the compilation and code profiling of this signal processing algorithm are shown in Table 4.1. To this end, we have used the software of LAB-STICC, SoftExplorer [LAB 06].

Conflicts		Cost (ms)	Data structures	Number of access
1	5	1,047,552	1	1,048,575
2	6	1,047,552	2	1,048,575
3	5	1,046,529	3	1,048,575
4	6	1,046,529	4	1,048,575
1	7	1,023	5	2,094,081
2	8	1,023	6	2,094,081
3	3	1,023	7	1,023
4	4	1,023	8	1,023

Table 4.1. *Conflicts and data structures of LMS dual-channel filter*

All data structures have the same size of 15,700 kB. The memory architecture has two memory banks with capacity of 47,100 kB. Memory banks can only store three data structures. On the target architecture, p is equal to 16 ms. Figure 4.2(a) shows the solution found by solving the ILP formulation using the solver Xpress-MP. Figure 4.2(b) illustrates the solution.

In the optimal solution, the data structures that are least accessed are allocated in the external memory. Thus, only auto-conflicts are open. The cost generated by this solution is formed by:

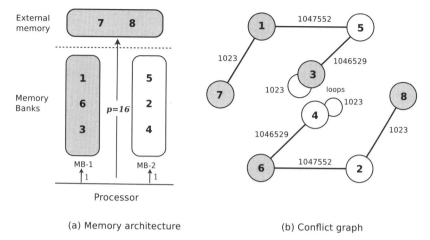

(a) Memory architecture   (b) Conflict graph

Figure 4.2. *An optimal solution for the example of MemExplorer*

Access time to memory banks: $\displaystyle\sum_{i=1}^{n}\sum_{j=1}^{m}\left(e_i x_{i,j}\right)$ = 8,382,462 ms

Access time to external memory: $\displaystyle p\sum_{i=1}^{n}\left(e_i x_{i,m+1}\right)$ = 32,736 ms

Access time saved by closed conflicts: $\displaystyle\sum_{k=1}^{o} y_k d_k$ = 4,190,208 ms

Hence, the total cost of the optimal solution is 4,224,990 ms.

4.4. Proposed metaheuristics

In this section, we describe the design of the different metaheuristics used for addressing this problem. Before presenting the metaheuristics for MemExplorer, we present the algorithms used for generating initial solutions, as well as two neighborhoods. Then, a tabu search-based approach is described with the two neighborhoods for exploring the solution space. At the end of this section, a variable neighborhood search-based approach hybridized with a tabu search-inspired method is also presented.

4.4.1. *Generating initial solutions*

Here, we present two ways for generating initial solutions. The first of these generates feasible solutions at random, and the second builds solutions using a greedy algorithm.

4.4.1.1. *Random initial solutions*

Algorithm 6 presents the procedure RandomMemex for generating random feasible initial solutions. At each iteration, a data structure is allocated to a random memory bank (or the external memory) provided that capacity constraints are satisfied.

4.4.1.2. *Greedy initial solutions*

GreedyMemex is a greedy algorithm for MemExplorer, this kind of algorithm makes locally optimal choices at each stage in the hope of finding the global optimum [BLA 05, COR 90]. Generally, greedy algorithms do not reach an optimal solution because they are trapped in local optima, but they are easy to implement and can provide initial solutions to more advanced approaches.

GreedyMemex is described in pseudo-code of Algorithm 7, where A is a permutation of the set $\{1, \ldots, n\}$ that models data structures, used for generating different solutions. Solution X^* is the best allocation found by the algorithm, where $(x_{i,j}^*)$ variables have the same meaning as in equation [4.1], and $f^* = f(X^*)$. Matrix G is used to assess the cost when data structures are moved to different memory banks or to the external memory. More precisely, $g_{i,j}$ is the sum of all open conflict costs produced by assigning data structure i to memory bank j. If data structure i is moved to external memory ($j = m + 1$), $g_{i,j}$ is the sum of all open conflict costs multiplied by p plus its access time multiplied by ($p - 1$). The numerical value of $g_{i,j}$ depends on the current solution because the open conflict cost depends on the allocation of the other data structures.

Output: $[X^*, f^*]$
Initialization:
Capacity used: $u_j \leftarrow 0, \forall j \in \{1, \ldots, m+1\}$
Allocation: $x^*_{ij} \leftarrow 0, \forall i \in \{1, \ldots, n\}, \forall j \in \{1, \ldots, m+1\}$
$f^* \leftarrow 0$
Assignment:
for $i \leftarrow 1$ **to** n **do**
    repeat
       | Generate j at random in $\{1, \ldots, m+1\}$
    until $u_j + s_i \leq c_j$;
    $x^*_{i,j} \leftarrow 1$
    $u_j \leftarrow u_j + s_i$
    Compute g_{ij}, the cost generated from allocating the data i to memory bank j
    $f^* \leftarrow f^* + g_{ij}$
end

Algorithm 6. *Pseudo-code for* `RandomMemex`

At each iteration, `GreedyMemex` completes a partial solution that is initially empty by allocating the next data structure in A. The allocation for the current data structure is performed by assigning it to the memory bank leading to the minimum local cost denoted by h^*, provided that no memory bank capacity is exceeded. The considered data structure is allocated to the external memory if no memory bank can hold it. Allocation cost f^* is returned when the all data structures have been allocated.

Input: $A \leftarrow \{a_1, \ldots, a_n\}$
Output: $[X^*, f^*]$
Initialization:
Capacity used: $u_j \leftarrow 0, \forall j \in \{1, \ldots, m+1\}$
Allocation: $x_{ij}^* \leftarrow 0, \forall i \in \{1, \ldots, n\}, \forall j \in \{1, \ldots, m+1\}$
$f^* \leftarrow 0$
Assignment:
for $i \leftarrow 1$ **to** n **do**
    $h^* \leftarrow \infty$ // (auxiliary variable for the
       partial greedy solution)
    for *j=1* **to** *m+1* **do**
        if $u_j + s_{a_i} < c_j$ **then**
           Compute g_{ij}, the cost for allocating data a_i to
           memory bank j
           if $g_{ij} < h^*$ **then**
              $b \leftarrow j$
              $h^* \leftarrow g_{ij}$
           end
        end
    end
    $x_{a_i,b}^* \leftarrow 1$
    $u_b \leftarrow u_b + s_{a_i}$
    $f^* \leftarrow f^* + h^*$ //total cost of the
    solution
end

Algorithm 7. *Pseudo-code for* `GreedyMemex`

`GreedyMemex` has a computational complexity of $\mathcal{O}(nm)$. Both algorithms require very few computational efforts, but return solutions that may be far from the optimality. However, these procedures are not used as standalone algorithms, but as subroutines, as called in Algorithm 8 for generating initial solutions for a tabu search-based procedure.

Input: A
Output: $[X^*, f^*]$
if $A \leftarrow \emptyset$ **then**
  | $(X^*, f^*) \leftarrow$ RandomMemex
else
  | $(X^*, f^*) \leftarrow$ GreedyMemex(A)
end

Algorithm 8. *Pseudo-code for* `InitialMemex`

4.4.2. *A tabu search procedure*

A tabu search method for MemExplorer is described in Algorithm 9, which is based on *TabuCol*, an algorithm for graph coloring described in [HER 87]. The main difference with a classic tabu search is that the size of the tabu list is not constant over time. This idea is discussed in [BAT 94] and also used in the work of Porumbel, Hao and Kuntz on the graph coloring problem [POR 09b]. In TabuMemex, the size of the tabu list NT is set to $a + NTmax \times t$ every $NTmax$ iterations, where a is a fixed integer and t is a random number in $[0, 2]$.

A pair (i, j) means that data structure i is in memory bank j. A move is a trio (i, h, j), this means that data structure i, which is currently in memory bank h, is to be moved to memory bank j. As a result, if the move (i, h, j) is performed, then the pair (i, h) is appended to the tabu list. Thus, the tabu list contains the pairs that have been performed in the recent past and it is updated on the first in first out (FIFO) basis.

The algorithm takes an initial solution X as input that can be returned by the procedure `InitialMemex`. Its behavior is controlled by some calibration parameters, such as the number of iterations, $Niter$, and the number of iterations for changing the size of the tabu list, $NTmax$. The result of this algorithm is the best allocation found X^* and its cost f^*.

Input: Initial solution X and number of neighborhood k
Output: $[X^*, f^*]$
Initialization:
Capacity used $u_j \leftarrow 0 \quad \forall j \in \{1, \ldots, m\}$
$NT \leftarrow NTmax$
$f^* \leftarrow \infty$
Iterative phase:
$Iter \leftarrow 0$
while $Iter < Niter$ **and** $f(X) > 0$ **do**
    $[X', (i, h, j)] \leftarrow$ Explore-Neighborhood-$\mathcal{N}_k(X)$
    $X \leftarrow X'$
    if $f(X') < f^*$ **then**
        $f^* \leftarrow f(X')$
        $X^* \leftarrow X'$
    end
    Update the tabu list with pairs (i, j) and (i, h)
    Update the size of tabu list NT
    $Iter \leftarrow Iter + 1$
end

Algorithm 9. *Pseudo-code for* TabuMemex

The iterative phase searches for the best solution in the neighborhood of the current solution. The neighborhood exploration is performed by calling Explore-Neighborhood-$\mathcal{N}_k(X)$, which calls the corresponding procedure with only one neighborhood used at a time. Two neighborhoods, denoted by $\mathcal{N}_0$ and $\mathcal{N}_1$ are considered; they are discussed in the following section. The fact that the new solution may be worse than the current solution does not matter because each new solution allows unexplored regions to be reached, and thus to escape local optima. This procedure is repeated for $Niter$ iterations, but the search stops if a solution without any open conflict, and for which the external memory is not used, is found. In fact, such a solution is necessarily optimal because the first and third terms of equation [4.3] are zero because no conflict cost has to be paid, and no data structure is in the external memory. Consequently, the objective function assumes its absolute minimum value, the second term of equation [4.3], and so is optimal. A new solution is accepted as the best one if its total cost is less than the current best solution.

This tabu search procedure will be used as a local search procedure in a VNS-based algorithm described in section 4.4.4.

4.4.3. *Exploration of neighborhoods*

In this section, we present two algorithms that explore two different neighborhoods for MemExplorer. Both of them return the best allocation (X') found along with the corresponding move (i, h, j) performed from a given solution X. In these algorithms, a move (i, h, j) is said to be non-tabu if the pair (i, j) is not in the tabu list. Algorithm 10 explores a neighborhood that is generated by performing a feasible allocation change of a single data structure.

Input: X
Output: $[X', (i, h, j)]$
Find a non tabu min cost move (i, h, j), such that $h \neq j$ and $u_j + s_i \leq c_j$
Build the new solution X' as follows:
$$X' \leftarrow X$$
$$x'_{i,h} \leftarrow 0$$
$$x'_{i,j} \leftarrow 1$$
$$u_j \leftarrow u_j + s_i$$
$$u_h \leftarrow u_h - s_i$$

Algorithm 10. *Pseudo-code for* Explore-Neighborhood-$\mathcal{N}_0$

Algorithm 11 presents the `Explore-Neighborhood-`$\mathcal{N}_1$. It explores solutions that are beyond $\mathcal{N}_0$ by allowing the creation of infeasible solutions before repairing them.

Input: X

Output: $[X', (i, h, j)]$

First phase: considering a potentially infeasible move

Find a non tabu min cost move (i, h, j), such that $h \neq j$

Build the new solution X' as follows:

   $X' \leftarrow X$

   $x'_{i,h} \leftarrow 0$

   $x'_{i,j} \leftarrow 1$

   $u_j \leftarrow u_j + s_i$

   $u_h \leftarrow u_h - s_i$

Second phase: repairing the solution

while $u_j > c_j$ **do**

   Find non tabu min cost move (l, j, b), such that $l \neq i$, $j \neq b$ and $u_b + t_l \leq c_b$

   Update solution X' as follows:

      $x'_{l,j} \leftarrow 0$

      $x'_{l,b} \leftarrow 1$

      $u_b \leftarrow u_b + s_l$

      $u_j \leftarrow u_j - s_l$

end

Algorithm 11. *Pseudo-code for* `Explore-Neighborhood-`$\mathcal{N}_1$

The first phase of `Explore-Neighborhood-`$\mathcal{N}_1$ performs a move that may make the current solution X' infeasible by violating the capacity constraint of a memory bank. However, this move is selected to minimize the cost of the new solution, and is not tabu. The second phase restores the solution not only by performing a series of reallocations for satisfying capacity constraints but by also trying to generate the minimum allocation cost. Then, it allows both feasible and infeasible regions to be visited successively. This way of using a neighborhood is referred to as *Strategic Oscillation* in [GLO 97].

4.4.4. *A variable neighborhood search hybridized with a tabu search*

Because both neighborhoods have their own utility (confirmed by preliminary tests), it seems clear that they should be used together in a certain way. The general variable neighborhood search [MLA 97] scheme is probably the most appropriate method to properly deal with several neighborhoods.

Algorithm 12 presents the VNS-based algorithm for MemExplorer. The number of neighborhoods is denoted by $kmax$, and the algorithm starts exploring $\mathcal{N}_0$ as $\mathcal{N}_0 \subset \mathcal{N}_1$.

The maximum number of iterations is denoted by $Nrepet$. Vns-Ts-MemExplorer, at each iteration, generates a solution X' at random from X. It copies the allocation of 60% of the data structures in the initial solution (60% of the data structures are selected randomly), and the GreedyMemex is used for mapping the remaining 40% of unallocated data structures for producing a complete solution X'.

This VNS algorithm relies on two neighborhoods. $\mathcal{N}_0$ is the smallest neighborhood, because it is restricted to feasible solutions only. If TabuMemex improves the current solution, it keeps searching for new solutions in that neighborhood. Otherwise, it does not accept the new solution and changes the neighborhood (i.e. by applying Explore-Neighborhood-$\mathcal{N}_1$ to the current solution).

Output: $[X^*, f^*]$
```
Initialization:
```
Generate A
$(X^*, f^*) \leftarrow$ `InitialMemex`(A)
$k \leftarrow 0$
```
Iterative phase:
```
$i \leftarrow 0$
while $i < Nrepet$ **do**
    `// Make a new initial solution` X `from` X^*
    $X \leftarrow 60\%$ of X^*, complete the solution with
    `GreedyMemex`
    Apply $(X', f') \leftarrow$ `TabuMemex`(X, k) using
    `Explore-Neighborhood-`$\mathcal{N}_k$
    if $f' < f^*$ **then**
        $X^* \leftarrow X'$
        $f^* \leftarrow f'$
        $i \leftarrow 0$
        $k \leftarrow 0$
    else
        if $k = kmax$ **then**
          $k \leftarrow 0$
        else
          $k \leftarrow k + 1$
        end
        $i \leftarrow i + 1.$
    end
end

Algorithm 12. *Pseudo-code for* `Vns-Ts-MemExplorer`

4.5. Computational results and discussion

This section presents the relevant aspects of the implementation of the algorithms. It also presents the information about the instances used to test our algorithms. Moreover, the results reached by our algorithms are presented and compared with the ILP formulation and the local search method.

4.5.1. *Instances used*

There are 43 instances for testing our algorithms, they are split into two sets of instances. The first one is a collection of real instances provided by LAB-STICC laboratory [LAB 11] for electronic design purposes. These instances have been generated from their source code using the profiling tools of SoftExplorer [LAB 06]. This set of instances is called LBS.

The second set of instances originates from the Center for Discrete Mathematics and Theoretical Computer Science (DIMACS) [POR 09a], a well-known collection of online graph coloring instances. The instances in Digital Mapping Camera (DMC) have been enriched by generating edge costs at random so as to create conflict costs, access times and sizes for data structures, and also by generating a random number of memory banks with random capacities. This second set of instances is called DMC.

Although real-life instances available today are relatively small, they will become larger and larger in the future as market pressure and technology tend to integrate more and more complex functionalities in embedded systems. Moreover, industrialists do not want to provide data about their embedded applications. Thus, we tested our approaches on current instances and on larger (but artificial) ones as well, for assessing their practical use for forthcoming needs.

4.5.2. *Implementation*

Algorithms have been implemented in C++ and compiled with gcc 4.11 on an Intel® Pentium IV processor system at 3 GHz and 1 gigabyte RAM.

In our experiments, the size of the tabu list is set every $NTmax = 50$ iterations to $NT = 5 + NTmax \times t$, where t is a real number selected at random in the interval $[0, 2]$. The maximum number of iterations has been set to $Niter = 50,000$.

For the initial solutions, we have used three different sorting procedures for permutation A of data structures. Then, we have three GreedyMemex algorithms: in the first algorithm, A is not sorted. In the second algorithm, A is sorted by decreasing order of the maximum conflict cost involving each data structure and in the third, A is sorted by decreasing order of the sum of the conflict cost involving each data structure. Hence, we have four initial solutions (random initial solutions and greedy solutions) and three ways of mapping the 40% of solution X' in VNS algorithm.

However, other tests showed that the benefit of using different initial solutions and different greedy algorithms to generate X' is not significant. In fact, this benefit is visible only for the most difficult instances with a low value of 1.2% on average, and for the other instances, VNS algorithm finds the same solutions, no matter the initial solution or greedy algorithm.

4.5.3. *Results*

The k-weighted graph coloring problem can be addressed by local search programming [VRE 03]. Thus, we have tested the local search on instances of MemExplorer, with the aim of comparing our algorithms with another heuristic approach. The result produced by the solver LocalSolver 1.0 [INN 10] is also reported.

The ILP formulation solved by Xpress-MP is used as a heuristic when the time limit of one hour is reached: the best solution found so far is then returned by the solver. A lower bound found by the solver was also calculated, but it was far too low for being useful.

The cost returned by Vns-Ts-MemExplorer is the best results obtained over all the combinations of different initial solutions and different greedy algorithms for generating a solution X'.

For a clear view of the difficulty, the instances have been sorted in non-decreasing order of number of conflicts. In Table 4.2, the first three columns show the main features of the instances (the source, the name, n: the number of data structures, o: the number of conflicts and m: the number of memory banks). The next two columns report the cost (in milliseconds) and CPU time (in seconds) of Vns-Ts-MemExplorer, the two following columns show the cost and CPU time of local solver and the last three columns display the results of the ILP model: lower bound, cost and CPU time.

4.5.4. *Discussion*

Vns-Ts-MemExplorer results are compared with local solver programming and the ILP formulation is solved by Xpress-MP. Bold figures in Table 4.2 represent the best-known solutions over all methods. In the ILP columns, the cost with an asterisk has been proved optimal by Xpress-MP. Vns-Ts-MemExplorer reaches the optimal solution for all of the instances for which the optimal cost is known. The optimal solution is known for 88% of the real electronic instances and for 31% of the DIMACS instances. Furthermore, Vns-Ts-MemExplorer always finds a better allocation cost than Xpress-MP. The number of best solutions reported by our approach is 38, compared to 16 with a local solver and 24 with the ILP model.

Instances			Vns-Ts-MemExplorer		Local solver		ILP		
Set	Name	$n\backslash o\backslash m$	Cost	Time	Cost	Time	Lower-bound	Cost	Time
LBS	compress	6\6\2	**511,232**	0.09	**511,232**	1.00	511,232	**511,232***	0.03
LBS	volterra	8\6\2	**1**	<0.01	**1**	1.00	1	**1***	0.33
LBS	adpcm	10\7\2	**224**	<0.01	**224**	1.00	224	**224***	0.08
LBS	cjpeg	11\7\2	**641**	0.2	**641**	1.00	641	**641***	0.05
LBS	lmsb	8\7\2	**3,140,610**	0.18	16,745,739	200	3,140,610	3,140,610*	0.50
LBS	lmsbv	8\8\2	**2,046**	<0.01	**2,046**	1.00	2,046	**2,046***	0.03
LBS	spectral	9\8\2	**640**	<0.01	**640**	1.00	640	**640***	0.03
LBS	gsm	19\17\2	**86,132**	0.34	**86,132**	1.00	86,132	**86,132***	0.06
LBS	lpc	15\19\2	**790**	0.42	**790**	200	790	**790***	0.19
DMC	myciel3	11\20\2	**377**	0.68	**377**	1.00	377	**377***	0.17
LBS	turbocode	12\22\3	**2,294**	0.43	**2,294**	300	2,294	**2,294***	0.34
LBS	treillis	33\61\2	**12.06**	1.43	**12.06**	200	12.06	**12.06***	0.28
LBS	mpeg	68\69\2	**786.5**	0.88	**786.5**	1,641	786.5	**786.5***	0.36
DMC	myciel4	23\71\3	**2,853**	1.94	2,930	1.00	2,853	**2,853***	16.30
DMC	mug88_1	88\146\2	**1,020**	6.33	1,379	3,596	1,020	**1,020***	31.23
DMC	mug88_25	88\146\2	**918**	7.00	1,263	3,483	918	**918***	13.71

Table 4.2. (Continued) Vns-Ts-MemExplorer, local solver and ILP results

Instances		Vns-Ts-MemExplorer		Local solver		ILP		
DMC queen5_5	25\160\3	**1,338**	2.47	**8,507**	140	1,338	**1,338***	1,616
DMC mug100_1	100\166\2	**2,652**	6.74	**2,788**	2,810	2,652	**2,652***	2,392
DMC mug100_25	100\166\2	**2,661**	5.40	**2,791**	1,198	2,661	**2,661***	1,165
DMC r125.1	125\209\3	**346**	8.94	361	31.00	260.33	**346**	3,600
LBS mpeg2enc	127\236\2	**32.09**	7.21	39.2	6.00	32.09	**32.09***	6.48
LBS mpeg2enc2	180\236\2	**32.09**	8.93	36.3	892	32.09	**32.09***	4.69
DMC myciel5	47\236\3	**2,990**	4.56	3,254	11	1,420.54	3,098	3,600
DMC queen6_6	36\290\4	**8,656**	14.63	9,029	1,940	4,213.43	8,871	3,600
LBS mpeg2	191\368\2	61,476.52	8.78	61,480.1	740	61,476.52	61,476.52*	12.00
DMC queen7_7	49\476\4	**13,951**	10.93	14,414	10.00	4,708.61	14,972	3,600
DMC queen8_8	64\728\5	**15,132**	10.48	15,389	7.00	482.77	17,183	3,600
LBS mpeg2x2	382\736\4	122,831.26	0.05	122,828.7	834	122,826.97	122,831.26	3,600
DMC myciel6	95\755\2	**9,135**	5.54	10,532	2,065	9,135	**9,135***	1,437
LBS ali	192\960\6	**7,951**	248.45	7,965	3,600	4,738.9	8,009	3,600
DMC myciel7	191\2,360\4	**3,347**	37.15	9,001	269	6.17	5,140	3,600
DMC zeroin_i3	206\3,540\15	**707**	26.80	757	2,936	15	962	3,600
DMC zeroin_i2	211\3,541\15	**575**	51.67	878	1,396	15	829	3,600
DMC r125.5	125\3,838\18	**20,502**	36.67	47,403	3,572	61.33	85,026	3,600
DMC mulsol_i2	188\3,885\16	1,470	91.59	**1,255**	3,299	31.61	5,722	3,600
DMC mulsol_i1	197\3,925\25	543	944.49	**520**	3,183	30	543	3,600

Table 4.2. (Continued) Vns-Ts-MemExplorer, local solver and ILP results

Instances		Vns-Ts-MemExplorer		Local solver			ILP	
DMC mulsol_i4	185\3,946\16	1,149	30.19	**1,047**	1,325	30.19	1,169	3,600
DMC mulsol_i5	186\3,973\16	**730**	53.17	2,022	1,383	15	1,840	3,600
DMC zeroin_i1	211\4,100\25	716	50.07	**497**	2,816	15	1,050	3,600
DMC r125.1c	125\7,501\23	**91,433**	44.55	266,463	3,210	15	289,868	3,600
DMC fpsol2i3	425\8,688\15	1,921	52.50	2,313	3,571	19.29	3,468	3,600
DMC fpsol2i2	451\8,691\15	**1,006**	89.38	1,813	3,563	30	2,059	3,600
DMC inithx_i1	864\18,707\27	**739**	204.28	1,154	3,590	15	2,878	3,600
Number of optimal solution		23		11			23	
Number of best solution		38		16			24	
Avgerage improvement on ILP:		35.29%		24%				
Avgerage CPU time (s):		48.27		1,349.44			1,881.95	

Table 4.2. *Vns-Ts-MemExplorer, local solver and ILP results*

In fact, on average, the ILP cost is improved by 35.29% using the VNS algorithm, whereas a local search can either improve the cost by 24% or gets worse by the cost of 71%. CPU time comparison of `Vns-Ts-MemExplorer` and ILP shows that our algorithm remains significantly faster than ILP in most cases. On average, the time spent by Xpress-MP is 1,700 times longer than the time spent by VNS algorithm. When no optimal solution is found with Xpress-MP, the lower bound on the objective value seems to be of poor quality, because it is 37% more than the best solution found on average. This suggests that after one hour of computation, the optimal solution would still require a very long time to be found or to be proven. For the instances for which the optimal solution is not known, the lower bound is often far from the best known solution. It is also important to note that the ILP performs well on small-size instances (up to 250 conflicts) because it benefits from very performant advances in its code (such as internal branch-and-cut, cut pool generation and presolver).

4.5.5. *Assessing TabuMemex*

In the VNS, the search is intensified by using `TabuMemex` as a local search procedure in the solution space. To assess the benefit of this strategy, we have tested our VNS with a classic tabu search method (i.e. without changing the size of the tabu list), and we have also tested `TabuMemex` with each neighborhood.

Table 4.3 shows the comparison between `Vns-Ts-MemExplorer` performances, a VNS variant with the classical tabu search and the tabu search alone with each of the two neighborhoods. The first two columns of Table 4.3 are the same as in Table 4.2, the next four columns report the cost value of each variant of the approach.

Instances		Vns-Ts M.	VNS with	Tabu search neighborhood	
Name	$n \backslash o \backslash m$	cost	classic tabu	$\mathcal{N}_0$	$\mathcal{N}_1$
compress	6\6\2	511,232	511,232	511,232	511,232
voltera	8\6\2	1	1	1	1
adpcm	10\7\2	224	224	224	224
cjpeg	11\7\2	641	641	641	641
lmsb	8\7\2	3,140,610	16,745,700	16,745,700	16,745,700
lmsbv	8\8\2	2,046	2,046	2,046	2,046
spectral	9\8\2	640	640	640	640
gsm	19\17\2	86,132	86,132	86,132	86,132
lpc	15\19\2	790	790	790	790
myciel3	11\20\2	377	2,167	377	377
turbocode	12\22\3	2,294	2,294	2,294	2,294
treillis	33\61\2	12.06	12.06	12.06	12.06
mpeg	68\69\2	786.5	790.88	786.5	790.5
myciel4	23\71\3	2,853	2,853	2,877	2,853

Table 4.3. *Intensity of some local search variants*

Instances		Vns-Ts M.	VNS with	Tabu search neighborhood	
Name	$n\backslash o\backslash m$	cost	classic tabu	$\mathcal{N}_0$	$\mathcal{N}_1$
mug88_1	88\146\2	1,020	1,068	1,036	1,020
mug88_25	88\146\2	918	1,095	918	950
queen5_5	25\160\3	1,338	1,342	1,342	1,342
mug100_1	100\166\2	2,652	2,735	2,901	2,662
mug100_25	100\166\2	2,661	2,734	2,661	2,661
r125.1	125\209\3	346	349	429	347
mpeg2enc	127\236\2	32.09	36.59	32.2	32.47
mpeg2enc2	180\236\2	32.09	38.48	32.2	33.22
myciel5	47\236\3	2,990	3,033	3,281	2,990
queen6_6	36\290\4	8,656	8,810	9,257	8,754
mpeg2	191\368\2	61,476.52	61,480.2	61,476.5	61,479.3
queen7_7	49\476\4	13,951	14,186	15,120	14,107
queen8_8	64\728\5	15,132	15,480	15,455	15,360
mpeg2x2	382\736\4	122,831.26	122,831.26	122,831.26	122,831.26
myciel6	95\755\2	9,135	9,706	9,135	9,135
ali	192\960\6	7,951	8,123	8,053	8,088
myciel7	191\2,360\4	3,347	3,741	4,116	3,548
zeroin_i3	206\3,540\15	707	754	2,233	791
zeroin_i2	211\3,541\15	575	632	954	607

Table 4.3. (Continued) Intensity of some local search variants

Instances		Vns-Ts M.	VNS with	Tabu search neighborhood	
Name	$n \backslash o \backslash m$	cost	classic tabu	$\mathcal{N}_0$	$\mathcal{N}_1$
r125.5	125\3,838\18	20,502	22,735	22,993	22,609
mulsol_i2	188\3,885\16	1,470	1,779	3,651	1,480
mulsol_i1	197\3,925\25	543	755	955	792
mulsol_i4	185\3,946\16	1,149	1,085	1,382	1,197
mulsol_i5	186\3,973\16	730	800	3,729	732
zeroin_i1	211\4,100\25	716	661	841	1,516
r125.1c	125\7,501\23	91,433	94,479	96,528	94,358
fpsol2i3	425\8,688\15	1,921	1,973	3,125	2,121
fpsol2i2	451\8,691\15	1,006	1,015	2,184	1,106
inithx_i1	864\18,707\27	739	820	1,698	850
Average worsening:			35%	56%	21%

Table 4.3. (Continued) Intensity of some local search variants

The costs reached by the other variants of VNS are worse in most cases, in fact, the solution cost of Vns-Ts-MemExplorer with classic tabu search is on average 35% higher than with TabuMemex; in addition, the tabu searches with each neighborhood (namely $\mathcal{N}_0$ and $\mathcal{N}_1$) are on average 56% and 21% worse than Vns-Ts-MemExplorer, respectively. This shows the benefit of the joint use of different neighborhoods and an advanced tabu search method.

4.6. Statistical analysis

In this section, we use a statistical test to identify differences in the performance of heuristics. In addition, we perform a post hoc paired analysis for comparing the performance between two heuristic approaches. This allows for identifying the best approach.

We have used the Friedman test [FRI 37] to detect differences in the performance of three heuristics (Vns-Ts-MemExplorer, local search, ILP formulation) using the results presented in Table 4.2.

As the results over instances are mutually independent and costs as well as CPU times can be ranked, we have applied the Friedman test for costs and CPU times. This allows us to compare separately (univariate model [CHI 07]) the performance in terms of solution quality and running time.

For each instance, the CPU times of the three approaches are ranked as follows. The smallest CPU time is ranked 1, the largest is ranked 3. If two CPU times are equal, their rank is computed as the average of the two candidate ranks (i.e. if two CPU times should be ranked 1 and 2, the rank is 1.5 for both). The same is performed for solution objective value.

The number of instances is denoted by r, the number of compared metaheuristic is denoted by q and the Friedman test statistic is denoted by Q, it is defined as follows:

$$Q = \frac{(r-1)(B_2 - rq\frac{(q+1)^2}{4}}{(A_2 - B_2)} \qquad [4.10]$$

where A_2 is the total sum of squared ranks and B_2 is the sum of squared R_i divided by q. R_i is the sum of ranks of metaheuristics i for all i in $\{1, \dots, q\}$.

The null hypothesis supposes that for each instance the ranking of the metaheuristics is equally likely. The null hypothesis is rejected at the level of significance α if Q is greater than the $1 - \alpha$ quantile of the $F_{(q_1, q_2)}$-distribution (Fisher–Snedecor distribution) with $q_1 = q - 1$ and $q_2 = (q-1)(r-1)$ degrees of freedom.

The test statistic Q is 21.86 for the running time, and 13.52 for the cost. Moreover, the value for the $F_{(2,84)}$-distribution with a significance level $\alpha = 0.01$ is 4.90. Then, we reject the null hypothesis for running time and cost at the level of significance $\alpha = 0.01$.

We can conclude that there exists at least one metaheuristic whose performance is different from at least one of the other metaheuristics. To know which metaheuristics are really different, it is necessary to perform an appropriate post hoc paired comparisons test.

4.6.1. *Post hoc paired comparisons*

As the null hypothesis of the Friedman test was rejected, we can use the following method for knowing if two metaheuristics are different [CON 99]. We say that two metaheuristics are different if:

$$|R_i - R_j| > \sqrt{\frac{2r(A_2 - B_2)}{(r-1)(q-1)}} t_{(1-\frac{\alpha}{2}, q_2)} \qquad [4.11]$$

where $t_{\left(1-\frac{\alpha}{2},q_2\right)}$ is the $1 - \frac{\alpha}{2}$ quantile of the t-distribution with $(r-1)(q-1)$ degrees of freedom.

For $\alpha = 0.01$, $t_{(0.095,84)}$-distribution is 2.64; then, the left-hand side of equation [4.11] for the running time is 20.06 and for the cost is 17.44. Table 4.4 summarizes the paired comparisons for the cost and the running time. The bold values in the table show that the metaheuristics are different.

Cost paired test			Running time paired test		
$|R_i - R_j|$	ILP	Local search	$|R_i - R_j|$	ILP	Local search
Vns-Ts-MemExplorer	**26**	**32.5**	Vns-Ts-MemExplorer	**42**	**45**
ILP	-	6.5	ILP	-	3
Critical value 17.44			Critical value 20.06		

Table 4.4. *Paired comparisons for MemExplorer*

The post hoc test shows that ILP and local search have the same performance in terms of solution cost and CPU time, whereas Vns-Ts-MemExplorer is the best approach in terms of solution cost and computational time.

4.7. Conclusion

In this chapter, an exact approach and a VNS-based metaheuristic are proposed for addressing a memory allocation problem. Vns-Ts-MemExplorer takes advantage of some features of tabu search methods initially developed for graph coloring, which is efficient as relaxing capacity constraints on memory banks leads to the k-weighted graph coloring problem. Vns-Ts-MemExplorer appears to be performing well because of its reasonable CPU time for large instances, and because it returns an optimal memory allocation for all instances for which the optimal cost is known.

These results allow one to hypothesize that the solutions found for the instances for which the optimal solution is unknown are of good quality. The improvements over a classic tabu search approach, such as the implementation of a variable tabu list, have a significant impact on solution quality. These features have `TabuMemex` exploring the search space efficiently.

`Vns-Ts-MemExplorer` achieves encouraging results for addressing the MemExplorer problem due to its well-balanced (intensification/diversification) search. The search is diversified by exploring the largest neighborhood when a local optimum is found, in addition, the local search method (`TabuMemex`) gives a more intensive search because of the significant improvements over a classic tabu search procedure. Using methods inspired by graph coloring problems can be successfully extended to more complex allocation problems for embedded systems, thereby accessing the gains made by using these methods to specific cases in terms of energy consumption. Moreover, it gives promising perspectives for using metaheuristics in the field of electronic design.

Finally, if the exact approach is suitable for today's applications, it is clearly not for tomorrow's needs. In fact, the best solution returned by the solver is generally very poor even after a long running time, and the quality of the lower bound is too bad to be at all helpful. The proposed metaheuristics appear to be suitable for the needs of today and tomorrow. The very modest CPU time compared to the exact method is an additional asset for integrating them to CAD tools, letting designers test different options in a reasonable amount of time.

The work presented in this chapter has been published in the *Journal of Heuristics* [SOT 11a] in 2011.

Chapter 5

Dynamic Memory Allocation Problem

This chapter deals with the last version of the memory allocation problem addressed in this book. The objective is to allocate data structures from a given application, to a given set of memory banks. In this variant, the execution time is split into time intervals. The memory allocation must consider the requirement and constraints at each time interval. Hence, the memory allocation is not static, it can be adjusted beause the application needs for data structures may change at each time interval.

After proposing an ILP model, we discuss two iterative metaheuristics for addressing this problem. These metaheuristics aim at determining which data structure should be stored in a cache memory at each time interval in order to minimize costs of reallocation and conflict. These approaches take advantage of metaheuristics designed for the previous memory allocation problem (see Chapters 3 and 4).

5.1. Introduction

The dynamic memory allocation problem, called *MemExplorer-Dynamic*, is presented in this chapter. This problem has a special emphasis on time performance. The general objective is to allocate data structures for a specific application to a given set of memory banks.

This problem is related to the data binding problems (section 1.3.3). For instance, in the work presented in [MAR 03], a periodical set of data structures must be allocated to memory banks; thus, the objective is to minimize the transfer cost produced by moving data structures between memory banks. Despite these similarities, there is no equivalent problem to the dynamic memory allocation problem.

The main difference between MemExplorer and this dynamic version of the memory allocation problem is that the execution time is split into T time intervals whose durations may be different. Those durations are assumed to be given along with the application. During each time interval, the application requires accessing a given subset of its data structures for reading and/or writing.

Figure 5.1 shows the memory architecture for MemExplorer-Dynamic, which is similar to that of a TI-C6201 device. It is composed of memory banks and an external memory. These memory banks have a limited capacity, and the capacity of external memory is large enough to allocate all data structures. The size of the data structures and the number of their accesses to them are both taken into account. Capacities of memory banks and the size of data structures are expressed in kilobytes (kB).

The processor accesses the data structure to perform the instructions of the application. As in MemExplorer, the access time of a data structure is its number of accesses multiplied by the transfer rate from the processor to memory banks or external memory. As before, the transfer rate from the processor to a memory bank is 1 ms, and the transfer time from processor to the external memory is p ms.

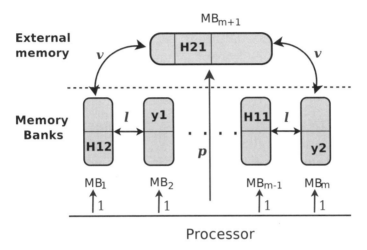

Figure 5.1. *Memory architecture for MemExplorer*

Initially (i.e. during time interval I_0), all data structures are in the external memory and memory banks are empty. The time required for moving a data structure from the external memory to a memory bank (and vice versa) is equal to the size of the data structure multiplied by the transfer rate v ms per kilobyte (ms/kB). The time required for moving a data structure from a memory bank to another is the size of data structure multiplied by the transfer time between memory banks, l ms/kB.

The memory management system is equipped with a direct memory access (DMA) controller that allows for a direct access to data structures. The time performances of that controller are captured with the numerical values of v and l. Therefore, the transfer times v and l are assumed to be less than the transfer time p.

The TI-C6201 device can access all its memory bank simultaneously, which allows for parallel data loading. As in the previous chapters, two conflicting data structures, namely a and b, can be loaded in parallel, provided that a and b are allocated to two different memory banks. If these data structures share the same memory bank, the processor has to access them sequentially, which requires twice the amount time if a and b have the same size.

Each conflict has a cost equal to the number of times that it appears in the application during the current time interval. This cost might be a non-integer if the application source code has been analyzed by a code-profiling software [IVE 99, LEE 02], based on the stochastic analysis of the branching probability of conditional instructions. This happens when an operation is executed within a while loop or after a conditional instruction such as if or else if (see the example of the non-integer cost presented in Chapter 3).

As before, a conflict between two data structures is said to be closed if both data structures are allocated to two different memory banks. In any other case, the conflict is said to be open.

Moreover, both particular cases, auto-conflicts and isolated data structures, are considered in this version of memory allocation problem.

The number of memory banks with their capacities, the external memory and its transfer rate, p, v and l, describe the architecture of the chip. The number of time intervals, the number of data structures, their size and access time describe the application, whereas the conflicts and their costs carry information on both the architecture and the application.

Contrarily to MemExplorer, where a static data structure allocation is searched for, the problem addressed in this chapter is to find a dynamic memory allocation, that is the memory allocation of a data structure may vary over time. Roughly speaking, we want the right data structure to be present in the memory architecture at the right time, while minimizing the efforts for updating memory mapping at each time interval.

MemExplorer-Dynamic is stated as follows: allocate a memory bank or the external memory to any data structure of the application for each time interval, so as to minimize the time spent in accessing and moving data structures while satisfying the memory banks' capacity.

The rest of the chapter is organized as follows. Section 5.2 gives an integer linear program formulation. Two iterative metaheuristics are then proposed for addressing larger problem instances in section 5.4. Computational results are then shown and discussed in section 5.5, and section 5.7 concludes this chapter.

5.2. ILP formulation for dynamic memory allocation problem

Let n be the number of data structures in the application. The size of a data structure is denoted by s_i, for all i in $\{1, \ldots, n\}$. n_t is the number of data structures that the application has to access during the time interval I_t, for all t in $\{1 \ldots, T\}$. $A_t \subset \{1, \ldots, n\}$ denotes the set of data structures required in the time interval I_t for all $t \in \{1, \ldots, T\}$. Thus, $e_{i,t}$ denotes the number of times that $i \in A_t$ is accessed in the interval I_t. The number of conflicts in I_t is denoted by o_t, and $d_{k,t}$ is the cost of conflict $(k, t) = (k_1, k_2)$ during the time interval I_t for all k in $\{1, \ldots, o_t\}$, k_1 and k_2 in A_t, and t in $\{1, \ldots, T\}$.

The allocation of data structures to memory banks (and to the external memory) for each time interval is modeled as follows. For all (i, j, t) in $\{1, \ldots, n\} \times \{1, \ldots, m+1\} \times \{1, \ldots, T\}$,

$$x_{i,j,t} = \begin{cases} 1, & \text{if and only if data structure } i \text{ is mapped} \\ & \text{to memory bank } j \text{ during time interval } I_t \\ 0, & \text{otherwise} \end{cases} \quad [5.1]$$

The statuses of conflicts are represented as follows. For all k in $\{1, \ldots, o_t\}$ and $t \in \{1, \ldots, T\}$,

$$y_{k,t} = \begin{cases} 1, & \text{if and only if conflict} \\ & k \text{ is closed during time interval } I_t \\ 0, & \text{otherwise} \end{cases} \quad [5.2]$$

The allocation change for a data structure is represented with the two following sets of variables. For all i in $\{1, \ldots, n\}$ and $t \in \{1, \ldots, T\}$, $w_{i,t}$ is set to 1 if and only if the data structure i has been moved from a memory bank $j \neq m + 1$ at I_{t-1} to a different memory bank $j' \neq m + 1$ during time interval I_t. For all i in $\{1, \ldots, n\}$ and $t \in \{1, \ldots, T\}$, $w'_{i,t}$ is set to 1 if and only if the data structure i has been moved from a memory bank $j \neq m+1$ at I_{t-1} to the external memory, or if it has been moved from the external memory at I_{t-1} to a memory bank during time interval I_t.

The cost of executing operations in the application can be written as follows:

$$\sum_{t=1}^{T} \left[\sum_{i \in A_t} \sum_{j=1}^{m} \left(e_{i,t} \cdot x_{i,j,t} \right) + p \sum_{i \in A_t} \left(e_{i,t} \cdot x_{i,m+1,t} \right) - \sum_{k=1}^{o_t} y_{k,t} \cdot d_{k,t} \right] \quad [5.3]$$

The first term in [5.3] is the access cost of all the data structures that are in a memory bank, the second term is the access cost of all the data structures allocated to the external memory and the last term accounts for the closed conflict cost.

The total cost of moving data structures between the intervals can be written as:

$$\sum_{t=1}^{T}\left[\sum_{i=1}^{n_t} s_i \cdot (l \cdot w_{i,t} + v \cdot w'_{i,t})\right] \qquad [5.4]$$

The cost of a solution is the sum of these two costs. Because $\sum_{i\in A_t}\sum_{j=1}^{m+1}\left(e_{i,t}\cdot x_{i,j,t}\right) = \sum_{i\in A_t}\left(e_{i,t}\right)$ is a constant term for all t in $\{1,\dots,T\}$, the cost function to minimize is equivalent to:

$$f = \sum_{t=1}^{T}\left[(p-1)\sum_{i\in A_t}\left(e_{i,t}\cdot x_{i,m+1,t}\right) - \sum_{k=1}^{o_t} y_{k,t}\cdot d_{k,t}\right.$$

$$\left. + \sum_{i\in A_t} s_i \cdot (l\cdot w_{i,t} + v\cdot w'_{i,t})\right] \qquad [5.5]$$

The ILP formulation of MemExplorer-Dynamic is then

Minimize f \qquad\qquad [5.6]

$$\sum_{j=1}^{m+1} x_{i,j,t} = 1 \ \forall i \in \{1,\dots,n\},\ \forall t \in \{1,\dots,T\} \qquad [5.7]$$

$$\sum_{i\in A_t}^{n} x_{i,j,t}s_i \le c_j \ \forall j \in \{1,\dots,m\},\ \forall t \in \{1,\dots,T\} \qquad [5.8]$$

$$x_{k_1,j,t} + x_{k_2,j,t} \le 2 - y_{k,t}\ \forall k_1,k_2 \in A_t,\ \forall j \in \{1,\dots,m+1\},$$

$$\forall k \in \{1,\dots,o_t\},\ \forall t \in \{1,\dots,T\} \qquad [5.9]$$

$$x_{i,j,t-1} + x_{i,g,t} \le 1 + w_{i,t}\ \forall i \in \{1,..,n\},$$

$$\forall j \ne g, (j,g) \in \{1,..,m\}^2,\ \forall t \in \{1,..,T\} \qquad [5.10]$$

$$x_{i,m+1,t-1} + x_{i,j,t} \le 1 + w'_{i,t}\ \forall i \in \{1,\dots,n\},$$

$$\forall j \in \{1,\dots,m\},\ \forall t \in \{1,\dots,T\} \qquad [5.11]$$

$$x_{i,j,t-1} + x_{i,m+1,t} \leq 1 + w'_{i,t} \ \forall i \in \{1,\ldots,n\},$$

$$\forall j \in \{1,\ldots,m\}, \ \forall t \in \{1,\ldots,T\} \qquad [5.12]$$

$$x_{i,j,0} = 0 \ \forall i \in \{1,\ldots,n\}, \ \forall j \in \{1,\ldots,m\} \qquad [5.13]$$

$$x_{i,m+1,0} = 1 \ \forall i \in \{1,\ldots,n\} \qquad [5.14]$$

$$x_{i,j,t} \in \{0,1\} \ \forall i \in \{1,\ldots,n\},$$

$$\forall j \in \{1,\ldots,m\}, \ \forall t \in \{1,\ldots,T\} \qquad [5.15]$$

$$w_{i,t} \in \{0,1\} \ \forall i \in \{1,\ldots,n\}, \ \forall t \in \{1,\ldots,T\} \qquad [5.16]$$

$$w'_{i,t} \in \{0,1\} \ \forall i \in \{1,\ldots,n\}, \ \forall t \in \{1,\ldots,T\} \qquad [5.17]$$

$$y_{k,t} \in \{0,1\} \ \forall k \in \{1,\ldots,o_t\}, \ \forall t \in \{1,\ldots,T\} \qquad [5.18]$$

Equation [5.7] enforces that any data structure is either allocated to a memory bank or to the external memory. Equation [5.8] states that the total size of the data structures allocated to any memory bank must not exceed its capacity. For all conflicts $(k,t) = (k_1, k_2)$, [5.9] ensures that data structure $y_{k,t}$ is set appropriately. Equations [5.10]–[5.12] enforce the same constraints for data structures $w_{i,t}$ and $w'_{i,t}$. The fact that initially all the data structures are in the external memory is enforced by [5.13] and [5.14]. Finally, binary requirements are enforced by [5.15]–[5.18].

This ILP formulation has been integrated in SoftExplorer. It can be solved for modest size instances using an ILP solver such as Xpress-MP [FIC 09]. Indeed, as MemExplorer is NP-hard, and then is MemExplorer-Dynamic.

5.3. An illustrative example

For the sake of illustration, MemExplorer-Dynamic is solved on an instance originating in the least mean square (LMS) dual-channel filter [BES 04], which is a well-known signal processing algorithm. This algorithm is written in C and is to be implemented on a TI-C6201 target. On that target, $p = 16$ ms, and $l = v = 1$ ms/kB.

The compilation and code profiling of the C file yields an instance with eight data structures having the same size of 15,700 kB; there are two memory banks whose capacity is 31,400 kB. For each time interval, Table 5.1 displays the data structures required by the application, the access time, the conflicts and their cost.

Intervals $t = 1, \ldots, 5$	Data structures $\{a_{1,t}, \ldots, a_{n_t,t}\}$	Conflicts $(a_{k_1,t}, a_{k_2,t})$	Cost $d_{k,t}$	Access time $e_{a_i,t,t}$
1	{ 1, 5, 2, 6 }	(1;5)	1,046,529	$e_{1,1} = e_{2,1} =$
		(2;6)	1,046,529	$e_{5,1} = e_{6,1} = 1,046,529$
2	{ 3, 4, 5, 6 }	(3;5)	1,046,529	$e_{3,2} = e_{5,2} =$
		(4;6)	1,046,529	$e_{4,2} = e_{6,2} = 1,046,529$
3	{ 1,5,7}	(1;7)	1,023	$e_{1,3} = 2,046$
		(1;5)	1,023	$e_{5,3} = e_{7,3} = 1,023$
4	{ 2,6,8 }	(2;6)	1,023	$e_{2,4} = 2,046$
		(2;8)	1,023	$e_{6,4} = e_{8,4} = 1,023$
5	{ 3,4 }	(3;3)	2,046	$e_{3,5} = e_{4,5} = 2,046$
		(4;4)	2,046	

Table 5.1. *Data about LMS dual-channel filter*

An optimal solution found by Xpress-MP [FIC 09] is shown in Figure 5.2. All data structures are in the external memory in initial interval I_0. In the first interval no conflict is open, only the moving cost is produced. A memory bank can only store two data structures. In the second time interval, data structures $1, 2, 3$ and 4 are swapped for avoiding access to data structures 3 and 4 from the external memory. Thus, no open conflict is produced, but a moving cost is generated. The memory allocation remains the same for the third interval, so a non-moving cost is produced but the conflict between data structures 1 and 7 is open. The optimal solution does not swap any data structures because they are used in the future intervals; in this way, the future moving cost is saved. In the fourth interval, data structures 5 and 2 are swapped, so no conflict is open, a moving cost is produced and the access time of data structure 8 is longer ($p \times e_{8,4}$). For the last time interval, the memory allocation remains the same, and the cost of the auto-conflicts is generated.

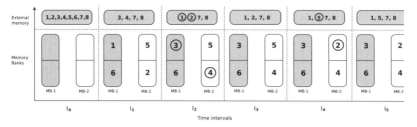

Figure 5.2. *An optimal solution for the example of MemExplorer-Dynamic*

The cost of this solution is 4,413,703 ms. Table 5.2 shows how this cost is dispatched. For each time interval, this table displays: the time spent by accessing data structures, the cost produced by moving data structures and the saved cost produced by closed conflicts.

Time interval (t)	1	2	3	4	5	Sum
Access time	4,186,116	4,186,116	50,127	19,437	4,092	8,445,888
Closed conflicts	2,093,058	2,093,058	1,023	2,046	0	4,189,185
Moving cost	62,800	62,800	0	31,400	0	157,000
Total cost	2,155,858	2,155,858	49,104	48,791	4,092	4,413,703

Table 5.2. *Cost of the optimal solution for the example of MemExplorer-Dynamic*

For larger instances (i.e. with more data structures, more conflicts, more memory banks and more time intervals), the proposed ILP approach can no longer be used. In the following section, two iterative metaheuristics are proposed for addressing MemExplorer-Dynamic.

5.4. Iterative metaheuristic approaches

5.4.1. *Long-term approach*

This approach takes into account the application requirements for the current and future time intervals. The long-term approach relies on addressing the general memory allocation (see Chapter 4). MemExplorer searches for a static memory allocation of data structures that could remain valid from the current time interval to the end of the last time interval. MemExplorer ignores the fact that the allocation of data structures can change at each time interval.

The long-term approach builds a solution iteratively, that is from time interval I_1 to time interval I_T. At each time interval, it builds a preliminary solution called the *parent solution*. The solution for the considered time interval is built as follows: the solution is initialized to the parent solution. Then, the data structures that are not required until the current time interval are allocated to the external memory.

At each time interval, the parent solution is selected from two candidate solutions. The candidate solutions are the parent solutions for the previous interval, and the solution to MemExplorer for the current interval. MemExplorer is addressed using a variable neighborhood search-based approach hybridized with a tabu search-inspired method (see Chapter 4).

The total cost of both candidate solutions is then computed. This cost is the sum of two subcosts. The first subcost is the cost that we would pay if the candidate solution were applied from the current time interval to the last time interval. The second subcost is the cost to be paid for changing the memory mapping from the solution of the previous time interval (which is known) to the candidate solution. Then, the candidate solution associated with the minimum total cost is selected as the parent solution.

The long-term approach is presented in Algorithm 13. A memory allocation is denoted by X, $X(a) = j$, means that data structure a is allocated to memory bank j. The solution X_t is associated with time interval I_t for all t in $\{1, \ldots, T\}$. The solution X_0 consists in allocating all the data structures of the application to the external memory.

The parent solution is denoted by P_t for the time interval I_t. The algorithm builds the solution X_t by initializing X_t to P_t, and the data structures that are not required until time interval I_t is moved to the external memory.

In the algorithm, M_t is the memory allocation found by solving the instance of MemExplorer built from the data for the time interval I_t. Then, a new instance of MemExplorer is solved at each iteration.

Algorithm 13 uses two functions to compute the total cost of a solution X. The first subcost is computed by the function `Access_Cost()`. This function returns the cost produced by a memory allocation X for a specified instances (data) of MemExplorer. The second subcost is computed by the function `Change_Cost($X_1, X_2$)`. It computes the cost of changing solution X_1 into solution X_2.

At each time interval I_t, the parent solution P_t is chosen between two candidates P_{t-1} and M_t. This parent solution produces the minimum total cost (comparing both the total cost $C_{P_{t-1}}$ and C_{M_t}).

At each iteration, Algorithm 13 updates the data and uses the same process to generate the time interval solution X_t for all t in $\{1, \ldots, t\}$.

Input: for each time interval $t \in \{1, \dots, T\}$ a set of data
structures A_t, a set of sizes of data structures S_t, a set
of conflicts between data structures K_t and a set of cost
of conflicts D_t.

Output: $X_1, \dots, X_T$ memory allocations for each time interval
and C the total cost of the solution.

```
//Initially all data structures are in the
external memory
```
$X_0(a) = m + 1$, for all $a \in \cup_{\alpha=1}^T A_\alpha$
$P_0 \leftarrow X_0$
for $t \leftarrow 1$ **to** T **do**
```
    //Updating data
```
$\quad$ $A = \cup_{\alpha=t}^T A_\alpha$, $A' = \cup_{\alpha=1}^t A_\alpha$, $E = \cup_{\alpha=t}^T E_\alpha$, $S = \cup_{\alpha=t}^T S_\alpha$,
$\quad$ $S' = \cup_{\alpha=1}^t S_\alpha$, $K = \cup_{\alpha=t}^T K_\alpha$, $D = \cup_{\alpha=t}^T D_\alpha$
```
    //Solving MemExplorer problem with current
    data
```
$\quad$ $M_t \leftarrow \text{MemExplorer}(A, E, S, K, D)$
```
    //Computing the total cost as the sum of two
    sub-costs
```
$\quad$ $C_{M_t} \leftarrow \text{Access\_Cost}(M_t, A, E, K, D) +$
$\quad$ $\text{Change\_Cost}(X_{t-1}, M_t, A', S')$
$\quad$ $C_{P_{t-1}} \leftarrow \text{Access\_Cost}(P_{t-1}, A, E, K, D) +$
$\quad$ $\text{Change\_Cost}(X_{t-1}, P_{t-1}, A', S')$
```
    //Choosing the parent solution
```
$\quad$ **if** $C_{M_t} < C_{P_{t-1}}$ **then**
$\quad$ | $\quad$ $P_t \leftarrow M_t$
$\quad$ **else**
$\quad$ | $\quad$ $P_t \leftarrow P_{t-1}$
$\quad$ **end**
```
    //Making the solution at time interval t
```
$\quad$ $X_t \leftarrow P_t$
$\quad$ **for** $a \notin A'$ **do**
$\quad$ | $\quad$ $X_t(a) = m + 1$
$\quad$ **end**
```
    //Computing the total cost of solution
```
$\quad$ $C \leftarrow C + \text{Access\_Cost}(X_t, A_t, E_t, K_t, D_t) +$
$\quad$ $\text{Change\_Cost}(X_{t-1}, X_t, A', S')$
end

Algorithm 13. *Long-term approach*

5.4.2. *Short-term approach*

This approach relies on addressing a memory allocation subproblem called MemExplorer-Prime. Given an initial memory allocation, this subproblem is to search for a memory allocation of the data structures that should be valid from the current time interval. This subproblem takes into account the cost for changing the solution of the previous time interval.

Input: for each time interval $t \in \{1, \ldots, T\}$ a set of data structures A_t, a set of sizes of data structures S_t, a set of conflicts between data structures K_t and a set of cost of conflicts D_t.

Output: $X_1, \ldots, X_T$ memory allocations for each time interval and C the total cost of the solution.

//Initially all data structures are in the external memory
$X_0(a) = m + 1$, for all $a \in \cup_{\alpha=1}^{T} A_\alpha$
for $t \leftarrow 1$ **to** T **do**
  | //Solve MemExplorer-Prime problem with current data
  | $X_t \leftarrow$ MemExplorer-Prime$(X_{t-1}, A_t, E_t, S_t, K_t, D_t)$
end

Algorithm 14. *Short-term approach*

MemExplorer-Prime is addressed for all time intervals. The data of this subproblem are the same as for MemExplorer. MemExplorer-Prime is stated as follows: for a given initial memory allocation for data structures, the number of capacitated memory banks and an external memory, we search for a memory allocation such that the time spent accessing data and the cost of changing allocation of these data are minimized. In this chapter, MemExplorer-Prime is addressed using a tabu search method similar to the method used by the long-term approach.

The short-term approach iteratively builds a solution for each time interval. Each solution is computed by taking into account the conflicts and data structures involved in the current time interval, and also by considering the allocation in the previous time interval. The short-term approach solves MemExplorer-Prime considering the allocation of the data structures of the previous interval as an initial allocation.

Algorithm 14 presents this approach. A solution X is defined as above, and it uses a function MemExplorer-Prime() for solving an instance of the problem MemExplorer-Prime where the initial solution is X_0.

At each iteration, the algorithm updates the data and the solution produced by MemExplorer-Prime() is taken as the time interval solution.

5.5. Computational results and discussion

This section presents the results obtained by the iterative approaches, which have been implemented in C++ and compiled with gcc 4.11 in Linux OS 10.04. They have been tested over two sets of instances on an Intel® Pentium IV processor system at 3 GHz with 1 GB RAM. The results produced by the iterative approaches are compared with the results of the ILP model and the local search method.

In practice, softwares such as SoftExplorer [LAB 06] can be used for collecting the data, but the code profiling is out of the scope of this work. We have used 44 instances to test our approaches. The instances of the set LBS are real-life instances that come from electronic design problems addressed in the LAB-STICC laboratory. The instances of DMC come from DIMACS [POR 09a], a well-known collection of graph coloring instances. The instances in DMC have been enriched by generating some edge costs at random to represent conflicts, access costs and sizes for data structures, the number of memory banks with random capacities and by dividing the conflicts and data structures into different time intervals.

For assessing the practical use of our approaches for forthcoming needs, we have tested our approaches on larger artificial instances, because the real-life instances available today are relatively small. In the future, the real-life instances will be larger and larger because designers tend to integrate more and more complex functionalities in embedded systems.

5.5.1. *Results*

For the experimental test, we have set the following values for transfer times: $p = 16$ (ms), and $l = v = 1$ (ms/kB) for all instances.

In Table 5.3, we compare the performances of the different approaches with the local search produced by LocalSolver 1.0 [INN 10] and with the ILP formulation solved by Xpress-MP, that is used as a heuristic when the time limit of one hour is reached: the best solution found so far is then returned by the solver.

We presented the instances sorted by non-decreasing sizes (i.e. by the number of conflicts and data structures). The first two columns of Table 5.3 show the main features of the instances: name, number of data structures, conflicts, memory banks and time intervals. The next two columns display the cost and the CPU time of the short-term approach in seconds (s). For the long-term approach, we show the best costs and its time reached in 12 runs, the standard deviation and the ratio between the standard deviation and average cost. For the local search, the cost and CPU time are also displayed. The following two columns report the cost and CPU time of the

ILP approach. The column "gap" reports the gap between the long-term approach and the ILP. It is the difference of costs of the long-term approach and the ILP divided by the cost of ILP. The last column indicates whether the solution returned by Xpress-MP is optimal.

The optimal solution is known only for the smallest instances. Memory issues prevented Xpress-MP and LocalSolver to address the nine largest instances. It is the same case for the LocalSolver, its memory prevents to address six of the largest instance.

Bold figures in the table are the best known solutions reported by each method. When the optimal solution is known, only three instances resist the long-term approach with a gap of at most 3%. From the 17 instances solved by Xpress-MP but without guarantee of the optimal solution, the ILP method finds six best solutions whereas the long-term approach improves 11 solutions, even sometimes up to 48%.

The last three rows of the table summarize the results. The short-term approach finds four optimal solutions and the long-term approach finds 14 of the 18 known optimal solutions. The local search reaches six optimal solutions. The long-term approach is giving the largest number of best solutions with an average improvement of 6% over the ILP method.

5.5.2. *Discussion*

The practical difficulty of an instance is related to its size (n, o), but it is not the only factor. The ratio between the total capacity of the memory bank and the sum of the sizes of data structures also plays a role. For example, instances `mug88_1dy` and `mug88_25dy` have the same size but the performance of Xpress-MP for the ILP formulation is very different.

Instances		Short-term		Long-term				Local search		ILP			
Name	$n \backslash o \backslash m$ T	Cost	(s)	Cost	(s)	Stand-Dev	Ratio	Cost	(s)	Cost	(s)	Gap	opt.
gsm_newdy	6\5\3 2	**7,808**	< 0.01	**7,808**	< 0.01	0.00	0.00	20,560	192	**7,808**	0.02	0.00	yes
compressdy	6\6\3 3	571,968	< 0.01	**342,592**	< 0.01	59,284	0.17	351,040	189	**342,592**	0.22	0.00	yes
volterrady	8\6\3 2	192	< 0.01	**178**	< 0.01	0.00	0.00	180	150	**178**	0.06	0.00	yes
cjpegdy	11\7\3 4	**4,466,800**	< 0.01	**4,466,800**	0.01	0.00	0.00	**4,466,800**	150	**4,466,800**	0.16	0.00	yes
lmsbvdy	8\8\3 3	**4,323,294**	< 0.01	**4,323,294**	< 0.01	1,352,052	0.31	4,347,870	150	**4,323,294**	0.11	0.00	yes
adpcmdy	10\8\3 3	49,120	< 0.01	**44,192**	0.01	0.00	0.00	50,648	150	**44,192**	0.11	0.00	yes
lmsbdy	8\8\3 3	54,470,706	0.01	**7,409,669**	0.29	1,146,369	0.23	8,458,246	150	**7,409,669**	0.48	0.00	yes
lmsbv01dy	8\8\3 4	4,399,847	< 0.01	**4,350,640**	< 0.01	388,819	0.09	4,402,865	150	**4,350,640**	0.38	0.00	yes
lmsbvdyexp	8\8\3 4	5,511,967	0.01	**4,367,024**	< 0.01	1,787,414	0.41	4,381,362	150	**4,367,024**	0.27	0.00	yes
spectraldy	9\8\3 3	44,912	< 0.01	15,476	0.01	4,393	0.25	**15,472**	150	**15,472**	0.27	0.00	yes
gsmdy	19\18\3 5	1,355,420	< 0.01	1,355,404	0.01	0.00	0.00	**1,355,390**	150	**1,355,390**	0.69	0.00	yes
gsmdycorr	19\18\3 5	494,134	< 0.01	**494,118**	0.04	0.00	0.00	**494,118**	150	**494,118**	0.77	0.00	yes
lpcdy	15\19\3 4	31,849	0.01	**26,888**	0.02	0.00	0.00	27159	150	**26,888**	0.32	0.00	yes
mycie13dy	11\20\3 4	6,947	< 0.01	3,890	0.01	457	0.11	4,156	150	**3,792**	1.44	0.03	yes
turbocodedy	12\22\4 4	3,835	< 0.01	3,246	0.13	158	0.05	3,801	150	**3,195**	23.09	0.02	yes
treillisdy	33\61\3 6	1,867	< 0.01	**1,806**	0.03	1	1.00	**1,806**	150	**1,806**	1.56	0.00	yes
mpegdy	68\69\3 8	11,108	< 0.01	10,630	0.13	110	0.01	11,334	300	**10,614**	6.21	0.00	yes
mycie14dy	23\71\4 7	16,277	< 0.01	8,847	0.94	121	0.01	10,580	150	8,611	3,600	0.03	no
mug88_1dy	88\146\3 6	27,521	0.02	25,543	5.17	126	0.00	26,046	150	25,307	3,600	0.01	no
mug88_25dy	88\146\3 6	24,641	0.16	24,310	5.87	178	0.01	25,333	150	24,181	1,197	0.01	yes
queen5_5dy	25\160\4 5	22,927	0.02	**15,358**	0.11	572	0.04	18683	150	15,522	3,600	-0.01	no
mug100_1dy	100\166\3 7	30,677	0.23	30,488	5.80	253	0.01	31,237	150	29,852	3,600	0.02	no

Table 5.3. *(Continued) Cost and CPU time for MemExplorer-Dynamic*

mug100_25dy	100\166\3	7	29,463	0.03	28,890	5.89	203	0.01	29,112	150	**28,448**	3,600	0.02	no
r125.1dy	125\209\4	6	37,486	0.14	**36,484**	2.93	24	0.00	39,504	150	36,489	3,600	-0.00	no
mycie15dy	47\236\4	6	26,218	0.03	24,162	0.11	336	0.01	28,421	150	**23,118**	3,600	0.05	no
mpeg2enc2dy	130\239\3	12	10,248	0.09	**9,812**	0.75	1	0.00	24,699	150	9,887	3,600	-0.01	no
queen6_6dy	36\290\5	10	31,710	0.04	**23,489**	0.35	219	0.01	30,499	150	24,678	3,600	-0.05	no
queen7_7dy	49\476\5	16	47,988	0.05	**37,599**	0.90	564	0.01	49,249	150	46,721	3,600	-0.20	no
queen8_8dy	64\728\6	24	73,091	0.13	**54,214**	2.10	195	0.00	76,322	150	86,270	3,600	-0.37	no
mycie16dy	95\755\3	11	70,133	0.16	65,716	11.21	670	0.01	68,573	150	**61,831**	3,600	0.06	no
alidy	192\960\7	48	135,682	0.58	64,696	1.46	2,124	0.03	**60,287**	3,600	65,882	3,600	-0.02	no
mycie17dy	191\2360\5	24	176,921	0.42	**163,676**	215.93	2,026	0.01	219,037	3,600	276,542	3,600	-0.41	no
zeroin_i3dy	206\3540\16	35	219,189	1.11	**212,138**	19.15	93	0.00	375,169	3,600	404,270	3,600	-0.48	no
zeroin_i2dy	211\3541\16	35	215,950	1.16	**210,464**	19.74	72	0.00	357,260	3,600	368,212	3,600	-0.43	no
r125.5dy	125\3838\19	38	379,162	1.12	**238,443**	561.98	1,297	0.01	382,624	3,600	430,900	3,600	-0.45	no
mulsol_i2dy	188\3885\17	39	238,724	0.86	**232,537**	20.69	160	0.00	419,936	3,600	-	-	-	no
mulsol_i1dy	197\3925\26	39	229,157	1.51	**222,410**	21.11	19	0.00	-	-	-	-	-	no
mulsol_i4dy	185\3946\17	39	240,439	0.96	**232,315**	17.67	149	0.00	462,025	3,600	-	-	-	no
mulsol_i5dy	186\3973\17	40	243,237	0.98	**236,332**	19.24	171	0.00	418,533	3,600	-	-	-	no
zeroin_i1dy	211\4100\26	41	236,435	1.59	**231,170**	22.72	34	0.00	-	-	-	-	-	no
r125.1cdy	125\7501\24	75	**413,261**	2.06	475,593	1,488	5,329	0.01	-	-	-	-	-	no
fpsol2i3dy	425\8688\16	87	528,049	2.50	**516,549**	189.39	398	0.00	-	-	-	-	-	no
fpsol2i2dy	451\8691\16	87	521,923	2.83	**509,834**	133.50	395	0.00	-	-	-	-	-	no
inithx_i1dy	864\18707\28	187	1,058,645	12.76	**1,038,331**	1,559	201	0.00	-	-	-	-	-	no
Number of optimal solutions			3		14				6		**18**			
Number of best solutions			4		33				6		24			
Average CPU time and gap				0.72		98.5				816.21			1,783.80	-0.06

Table 5.3. *Cost and CPU time for MemExplorer-Dynamic*

In most cases, the proposed metaheuristic approaches are significantly faster than Xpress-MP and LocalSolver, with the short-term approach being the fastest approach. The short-term approach is useful when the cost of reallocating data structures is small compared to conflicts costs. In such a case, it makes sense to focus on minimizing the cost of the current time interval without taking future needs into account, because the most important term in the total cost is due to open conflicts. The long-term approach is useful in the opposite situation (i.e. moving data structures is costly compared to conflict costs). In that case, anticipating future needs makes sense as the solution is expected to undergo very few modification over time. Table 5.3 shows that the architecture used and the considered instances are such that the long-term approach returns a solution of higher quality than the short-term approach (except for r125.1cdy), and then emerges as the best method for today's electronic applications, as well as for future needs.

5.6. Statistical analysis

As in the previous chapter, we used the Friedman test [FRI 37] to identify differences in the performance of iterative approaches, local search and ILP solution. The post hoc paired test is also performed to identify the best approach.

For this test, we use the results presented in Table 5.3, because the results over instances are mutually independent. Thus, costs as well as CPU times can be ranked as in Chapter 4, and the Friedman test statistic is denoted by Q and it is defined as in equation [4.10].

The test statistic Q is 18.85 for the objective function, and 111.18 for the CPU time. Moreover, the value for the $F_{(3,102)}$-distribution with a significance level $\alpha = 0.01$ is 3.98.

Then, we reject the null hypothesis for cost and running time at the level of significance $\alpha = 0.01$.

Hence, we conclude that there exists at least one metaheuristic whose performance is different from at least one of the other metaheuristics.

5.6.1. *Post hoc paired comparisons*

We use the same post hoc test of section 4.6 for comparing the performance between two metaheuristics. Table 5.4 summarizes the paired comparisons for the cost and running time using an $\alpha = 0.01$; thus, $t_{(0.095,102)}$-distribution is 2.63, and the left-hand side of equation [4.11] for the running time is 13.21 and the cost is 21.26. Data given in bold highlights the best obtained results.

Cost paired test				Running time paired test			
$\|R_i - R_j\|$	Short-term	ILP	Local search	$\|R_i - R_j\|$	Short-term	ILP	Local search
Long-term	**51**	6	**39**	Long-term	**33.5**	**43.5**	**44**
Short-term	-	**45**	12	Short-term	-	**77**	**77.5**
ILP	-	-	**33**	ILP	-	-	0.5
Critical value = 21.26				Critical value = 13.21			

Table 5.4. *Paired comparisons for MemExplorer-Dynamic*

The post hoc test shows that the ILP and the long-term approach have the same performance in terms of solution cost, but the long-term approach is better than the ILP in terms of running time. The long-term approach outperforms the local search and short-term approach. On the other hand, the short-term approach is the best approach in terms of running time and its performance in terms of cost is equal to the one of local search. Finally, ILP and local search have the same performance in terms of running time.

5.7. Conclusion

This chapter presents an exact approach and two iterative metaheuristics, based on the general memory allocation problem. Numerical results show that the long-term approach gives good results in a reasonable amount of time, which makes this approach appropriate for today's and tomorrow's needs. However, the long-term approach is outperformed by the short-term approach in some instances, which suggests that taking the future requirements and aggregating the data structures and conflicts of the forthcoming time interval might not always be relevant. In fact, the main drawback of this approach is that it ignores the potential for updating the solution at each iteration.

The work discussed in this chapter has been presented at the European Conference on Evolutionary Computation in Combinatorial Optimization (EVOCOP) [SOT 11c].

Chapter 6

MemExplorer: Cases Studies

6.1. The design flow

This section first introduces the target architecture used (i.e. the processor and the memory hierarchy) and then presents the estimation flow (parameters extraction), in particular, the determination of the memory conflict graph (MCG) that allows us to compute the cost of each memory access by using the cost library.

6.1.1. *Architecture used*

Figure 6.1 presents the generic architecture used in the modeling scheme. This architecture is composed of one processor, n on-chip memory banks (with $n \geq 0$) that can be accessed by the processor to load/store its data and one external memory that can also store data (typically, the data that cannot be stored into the on-chip memory).

This type of memory architecture is often used in embedded systems because the scratchpad memories have the advantage of consuming less power than cache memories. On the one hand, the n on-chip memory banks are fast but small-sized memories, mostly a few hundred kilobytes. On the other hand, the external memory is far larger but significantly slower. Indeed, the typical access time of this kind of memory is some milliseconds, whereas on-chip memory access time is of a few nanoseconds. These features play a key role in memory mapping: if the size of a data structure exceeds the on-chip memory bank capacity, then it has to be allocated to the external memory. Furthermore, even a data structure whose size is less than the on-chip memory bank capacity may be allocated to the external memory bank if the available on-chip memory bank capacity is not large enough.

Besides memory capacity, memory access time is also an important parameter: a data structure that is often accessed by the application should be placed in the on-chip memory bank otherwise the whole application execution could be delayed.

These features (memory capacity and access time) are stored in a memory library for each memory type. This library enables MemExplorer users to get the best memory mapping to fit their architecture.

6.1.2. MemExplorer design flow

The first step in the MemExplorer design flow is to extract two types of information from the application. The first type is the size (in byte) of all data structures used in the application and the second type is the cost of all conflicts involving the data structures. These extractions are performed automatically from the application source code, this is achieved by a modified version of a GNU Compiler Collection (GCC) compiler front end.

The MemExplorer design flow is shown in Figure 6.2.

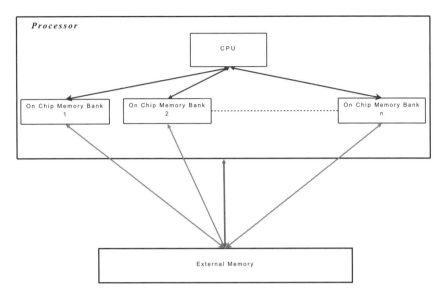

Figure 6.1. *Generic architecture*

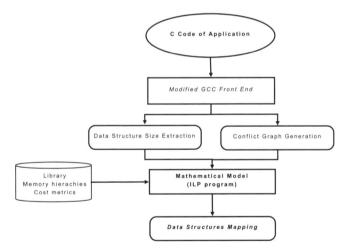

Figure 6.2. *MemExplorer design flow*

The entry point of the MemExplorer flow is a C source code provided by the user. This code is parsed by the modified front end of GCC 4.2. This parsing yields the size of each data structure (pointers are also taken into account) and the conflict graph that points out which structures are accessed in parallel. These parallel accesses generate access conflicts if the structures are mapped into the same on-chip memory bank or are both mapped into the external memory, or if one data structure is allocated an on-chip memory bank and the other data structure is allocated the external memory.

For each type of memory hierarchy, the library contains the delay costs generated by the access conflicts. Of course, these costs depend on the memory type used (on-chip or off-chip, shadow random access memory (SRAM), synchronous dynamic random access memory (SCRAM) and so on); they also depend on the processor used since the memory (on-chip or off-chip) access time differs from one processor to another. When the conflict graph and the data structure size extraction are completed, the mathematical model uses this information and the cost metric library (as presented in Figure 6.2) in order to generate the optimal data structure mapping.

6.1.3. *Memory conflict graph*

This section introduces some small examples to illustrate the MCG extraction and its associated semantic.

Figure 6.3 shows a brief application where only four data structures are used. These structures (which are arrays) are accessed in reading and/or writing mode.

```
Function1 (tab_res)
{
short tab1[20], tab2[10];
int tab_temp[20], tab_res[20];

        tab_temp[2]=tab1[5] x tab2[9];
        tab_res[11]= tab2[1];
        tab_temp[7]= tab1[4] x 2;
}
```

Figure 6.3. *Code Example 1*

The first step taken by the front end (developed from GCC 4.2) is to extract the size of each data structure used in the application. This extraction is performed from the C code provided by the user. In the example provided (see Figure 6.3), we have to extract the size of the four data structures: `tab1`, `tab2`, `tab_res`, `tab_temp`. The first two data structures in this application are structures of `short` type, where a `short` is assumed to be a 2-byte word. Thus, `tab1` has 20 elements of 2 bytes so its size is 40 bytes (the size of `tab2` is 20 bytes). `tab_res` and `tab_temp` have a size of 80 bytes, so all the elements of these structures are represented using 4 bytes; an `int` element being coded in 32 bits in this example (the `int` size depends on the data bus size of the processor used).

The second step consists of analyzing all the possible access conflicts (in writing and/or reading mode) between the different data structures: these conflicts appear in the MCG. Figure 6.4 shows the MCG for the first example. It can be seen that `tab1` and `tab2` are conflicting and that this conflict has a cost of one. The cost of this conflict corresponds to the memory accesses performed in the first instruction of the provided example and we suppose that the load accesses are realized first. The cost carried by the arcs represents the maximum number of access conflicts. Similarly, we can determine the cost of each arc of the MCG. Finally, we can determine that `tab1` and `tab_res` are conflicting with an associated cost of one and that `tab2` and `tab_temp` are also in conflict with the same cost.

This first example shows a very simple case where no loops and/or control structures (`if`, `else`, `switch` and so forth) are used. If such control or loop structure is used in the application, we undertake the following. Each liner instruction block (LIB) is considered separately and defines the memory conflicts by taking into account the iteration numbers (for the loops) and the probability to take each branch of control structures (for the `if`, `else`...). The second example (see Figure 6.5) shows a part of this rule application when there are control structures in the C code.

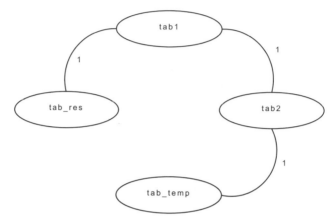

Figure 6.4. *Memory conflict graph: Example 1*

```
Function1 (i,tab_res)
{
short tab1[20], tab2[10];
int tab_temp[20], tab_res[20];

    if (i==2)
    {
        tab_temp[2]=tab1[5] x tab2[9];
        tab_res[11]= tab2[1];
        tab_temp[14]=tab1[6] x 4;
    }
    else
    {
        tab_temp[2]=tab1[3] x tab2[0];
    }
}
```

Figure 6.5. *Code Example 2*

In Figure 6.6, we can see that there are three possible conflicts: the first one between `tab1` and `tab_res` with a cost of 0.5, the second between `tab2` and `tab_temp` with the same cost and the last one between `tab1` and `tab2` with a cost of one. This last conflict is twice more costly than the others because a conflict exists between these two data not only in the if branch but also in the else one. So, as the probability to take each branch of the control structure is the same in this example (by default, the two branches have the same probability), each conflict (in the if and the else branches) can occur one time with a probability of 0.5. In conclusion, each conflict has a cost of 0.5, so the addition of these costs is carried by one arc whose cost is one. The MemExplorer user can change the execution probabilities of each control branch by using pragma inserted into the C code. These pragma are used by our tool but are not taken into account during the compilation step (as with code comments).

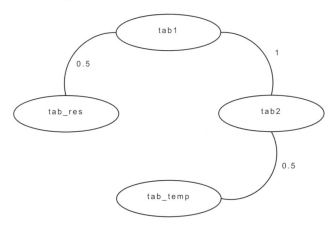

Figure 6.6. *Memory conflict graph: Example 2*

Finally, the third example (see Figure 6.7) shows an application using loops and control structures.

In Figure 6.8, there are three memory conflicts: the first one between tab1 and tab2 with a cost of 7.5, the second between tab2 and tab_temp with the same cost and the third conflict between tab1 and tab_res with a cost of 12.5. Each cost is computed by using both the iteration number of loops, in which the conflicts are generated, and the probability to execute the branch control. In this example, the probability to execute the `if` branch is equal to 0.75 (normalized to one) because the user annotated the C code thus the probability to execute the `else` branch is then equal to 0.25 (MemExplorer computes the `else` probability by subtracting 0.75 from one so, the user does not need to annotate the `else`). Furthermore, the iteration number of the first loop is equal to 10 so the first conflict between `tab1` and `tab2` is computed as follows:

$$\text{Conflict Cost} = 0.75 \times 10 = 7.5$$

```
Function1 (tab_res)
{
short tab1[20], tab2[10];
int tab_temp[20], tab_res[20];
int i=0;
    #pragma probability 0.75
    if (i==2)
    {
        for(i=0;i<10;i++)
        {
            tab_temp[i]=tab1[i] x tab2[i];
            tab_res[i]= tab2[i];
            tab_temp[i]=tab1[i] x 4;
        }
    }
    else
    {
        for(i=0;i<20;i++)
            tab_temp[i]=tab_res[i] x tab1[i];
    }
}
```

Figure 6.7. *Code Example 3*

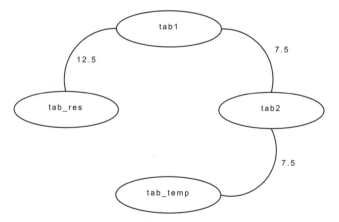

Figure 6.8. *Memory conflict graph: Example 3*

A node in the graph (which represents a data structure) can only be connected to another node with a single arc. The cost of that arc is computed as the sum of all the costs associated with identical conflicts over all LIB of the C code. As similar conflicts can exist in several C functions of the same application, we take into account the call number of each of these functions to weight the arc values of the MCG.

6.2. Example of MemExplorer utilization

Here, we give a step-by-step account for MemExplorer to obtain a data mapping. The first example is a classical signal processing application called a FIR filter. In this application, we have three data structures to map into the memory hierarchy. Two of them called samples and coefficients are de noted by H and X; the result of the filter is denoted by Y. Each data structure is composed of 1,024 elements of 32 bits each. Structures X and H are accessed at the same time to increase parallelism so if one wants to decrease the conflict cost, one has to map them into two different memory banks. The output Y can be mapped into any memory bank because it is not accessed in parallel with any other data structure. The first step to take in using the MemExplorer tool is to choose the C code to be analyzed. Figure 6.9 shows the edition of the C code for the FIR filter.

Once the C code has been analyzed, a XML file is generated allowing the user to verify if all the codes have been processed (see Figure 6.10).

The next step is to define the MCG; this graph is generated by using the power estimation tab (see Figure 6.11). In this tab, one must choose the C6201 processor (in the future, more processors will be available), the data model for the prediction model (this allows taking into account the data accesses), the frequency (only used for power estimation in SoftExplorer), the mapped memory mode (use of the internal memory bank) and finally a coarse estimation for the prediction tab. Any other configuration will not lead to generating the conflict graph properly.

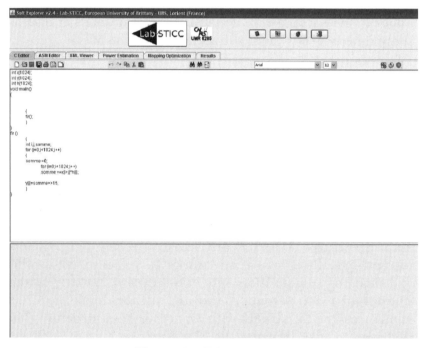

Figure 6.9. *Edition screen*

Then, we must choose the initial memory mapping file generated at the same time as the MCG (see Figure 6.12). In fact, the initial memory mapping file considers that all the data structures are in the same memory bank in order to generate the MCG.

The next step is to choose the optimization method that the user wants to use (see Figure 6.13). Four different methods are currently available: a tabu search method, Evocol (these two methods do not take into account the memory size to obtain the best memory mapping, so they are not very useful for this purpose), Vns-TS and finally the integer programming (with GNU Linear Programming Kit (GLPK) solver).

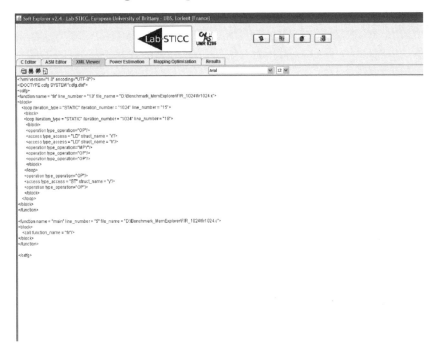

Figure 6.10. *XML screen*

Figure 6.14 shows the result for the FIR filter when Vns-TS is called. We can see that as mentioned at the beginning of this chapter, two data structures of 1,024 elements of 32 bits are stored in memory bank 1 (8,192 bytes of 32,768 bytes), one structure is in bank 0 and thus nothing is in the external memory (named 2 here).

Finally, Figure 6.16 presents the results returned by the GLPK-based method. The solution found with this method shows that our result is optimal and identical to the one returned by Vns-TS.

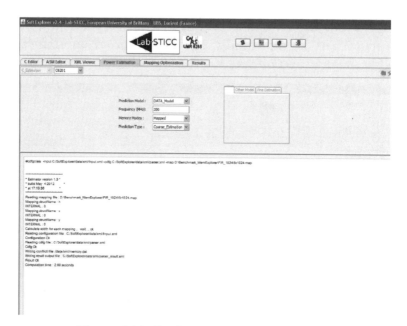

Figure 6.11. *Conflict graph generation screen*

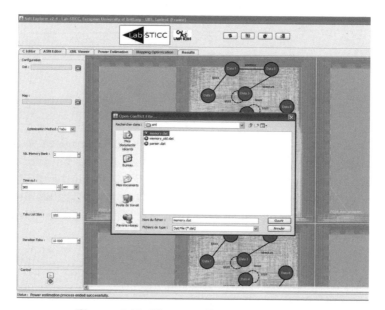

Figure 6.12. *Mapping file selection screen*

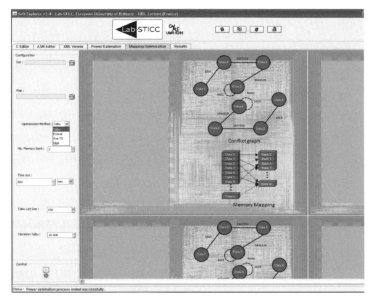

Figure 6.13. *Optimization tab screen*

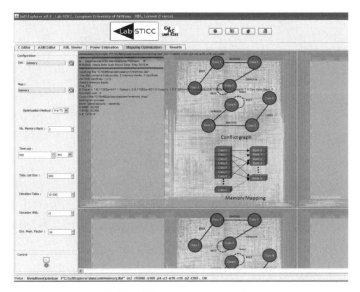

Figure 6.14. *Vns-TS mapping optimization screen*

```
Bank       UsedCapicity       capacity
0 4098 32768
1 8192 32768
2 0 1e+010
```

Figure 6.15. *Vns-TS mapping optimization output*

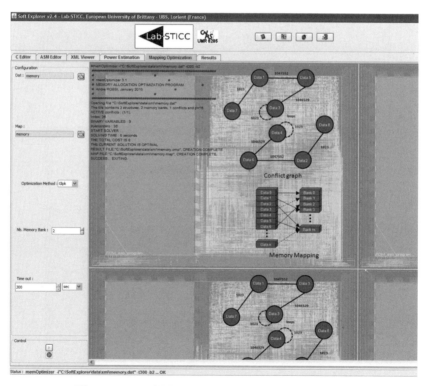

Figure 6.16. *GLPK mapping optimization Screen*

```
THE TOTAL COST IS 0
THE CURRENT SOLUTION IS OPTIMAL
RESULT FILE: "C:\SoftExplorer\data\xml\memory.omp",
CREATION COMPLETE.
MAP FILE :"C:\SoftExplorer\data\xml\memory.map",
CREATION COMPLETE.
SUCCESS... EXITING
```

Figure 6.17. *GLPK mapping optimization output*

Chapter 7

General Conclusions and Future Work

This chapter concludes the book. First, we summarize the different versions of the memory allocation problem and discuss the diversification and intensification of metaheuristics designed for these versions. Then, we present the main conclusions and perspectives emerging from this work.

7.1. Summary of the memory allocation problem versions

In this book, we have introduced four versions of the memory allocation problem. The general objective of these problems is focused either on the memory management or on the data assignment in embedded systems because both have a significant impact on the main cost metrics, such as cost, area, performance and power consumption. These cost metrics are the main features taken into account by designers in industry and by customers, requiring the integration of an increasing number of functionalities.

The first version of the memory allocation problem is concerned with hardware optimization; it is focused on the memory architecture (the memory architecture can be composed of memory banks, an external memory, scratchpads, etc.) of the application. The three remaining problems are related to the data binding; it searches for an optimal memory allocation of data structures to a fixed memory architecture. Table 7.1 summarizes the main characteristics, constraints and objective function of these problems as well as metaheuristics designed for them.

All versions of the memory allocation problem are $\mathcal{NP}$-hard problems. For each version, the number of constraints increases, and the objective function and the characteristics of the memory allocation problems change. Thus, for each version, the complexity in the memory allocation problem increases. Differences between the first version problem and the last two versions are noticeable.

The first problem searches for the minimum number of memory banks for which all non-auto-conflict are closed and this problem can be modeled as the vertex coloring problem. In the second problem, the number of memory banks is fixed and we search for an optimal memory allocation of data structures to memory banks to minimize the cost produced by the open conflicts; this problem is equivalent to the k-weighted graph coloring problem. In the third problem, in addition to a fixed number of memory banks, the capacity of memory banks is limited. The memory architecture has an external memory, which has enough capacity to store all data structures, but the access to this external memory is p ms slower than to memory banks. Moreover, the size of the data structures and the number of accesses are taken into account. The main difference between the last problem and the general problem is that the time is split into time intervals. Allocation of data structures can change at each time interval, so we must consider the cost for moving them. Thus, we search for a memory allocation for each time interval to minimize the total time by accessing and moving data structures.

As the complexity of the version problems increases, we use more sophisticated methods. These methods have reached good results. The following section analyzes these approaches in terms of intensification and diversification.

7.2. Intensification and diversification

For addressing the remaining three problem versions, we have proposed exact mathematical models and metaheuristic approaches. These metaheuristics are inspired by the methods originally designed for the vertex coloring problems. In this section, we examine the proposed approaches in terms of intensification and diversification.

7.2.1. *Metaheuristics for memory allocation problem with constraint on the number of memory banks*

We have proposed two metaheuristics to tackle this problem. The first metaheuristic is a tabu search method called `Tabu-Allocation` and the second metaheuristic is an evolutionary algorithm called `Evo-Allocation`.

7.2.1.1. *Tabu-Allocation*

The diversification in this method is due to the presence of the tabu list and mainly due to the dynamic size of this tabu list, it is relative to Reactive Tabu Search [BAT 94]. This allows us to explore new neighborhoods and escape from local optimum. For example, using a static size of the tabu list, the instance `mpeg2enc` reaches a cost of 33.22 ms, and using a dynamic size the method reaches a cost of 32.09 ms, that is the method improves the solution by 3.4% by using a dynamic size of tabu list.

Problem version	Objective	Features	Methods
Hardware optimization			
– Unconstrained	Search for the minimum Number of memory banks	– All non-auto-conflicts have to be closed	Upper bounds on χ ξ, ζ and η
Data binding. Allocating data structures to memory banks			
– Constraint on the number of memory banks	Minimize the total cost of open conflicts	– Number of memory banks fixed	ILP Local search Tabu search Evolutionary Algorithm
General	Minimize the total time spent accessing data structures	– Number of memory banks fixed – Capacitated memory banks – External memory (p ms) – Sizes of data structures – Number of accesses to data structure	ILP Local-search VNS Tabu-search
Dynamic	Minimize the total time spent accessing and moving data structures	– Time intervals – Number of memory banks fixed – Capacitated memory banks – External memory (p ms) – Transfer rates v and l – Sizes of data structures – Number of accesses to data structure	ILP Local-search Short-term Long-term

Table 7.1. *Summary of the memory allocation problem versions*

The method intensifies the search by accepting an enhanced solution as initial one; thus, its neighborhood is explored to find a better solution.

7.2.1.2. *Evo-Allocation*

Three motives guarantee the diversification in the population of this approach. The first motive is because the algorithm accepts an offspring (new solution) if the distance to its parents is greater than a fixed threshold. The objective is to avoid having too many solutions with similar characteristics. The second reason is the random selection of several parents to the crossover; thus, it allows us to cross good and bad parents to produce offsprings with new characteristics. The last reason is the criterion of statistical variance of solution costs to update the population; this allows refreshing the population. For example, the method reaches the cost of 762 ms for the instance `r125.5` without the statistic variance condition, and it reaches the cost of 734 ms with this criterion, that is the solution is improved by 3.7% using the statistical variance for updating the population.

The intensification of `Evo-Allocation` is due to three reasons. The first reason is the crossover function, as it takes the best allocations of data structures from each solution to produce a new one; so the good characteristics of parents solutions are kept in the population. The second reason is the tabu search (with a dynamic size of tabu list) used to improve the quality of the offspring. The last reason is presented in the way of updating the population that replaces the worst solutions with new solutions.

7.2.2. *Metaheuristic for general memory allocation problem*

For this problem, we have proposed a variable neighborhood search based approach hybridized with a tabu search inspired method, that is `Vns-Ts-MemExplorer`.

There are three main motives that assure the diversification in this method. The current solution is perturbed, so this forces us to explore new neighborhoods and to find new good solutions. Another important subject to diversification is the second neighborhood $\mathcal{N}_1$, which allows the method to explore prohibited neighborhoods. Thus, the method explores neighborhoods beyond the usual ones and it allows the method to escape easily from local optimums. The last motive is the combination of the two neighborhoods. This combination leads to a better cover of the search space. If we use a single neighborhood, either $\mathcal{N}_0$ or $\mathcal{N}_1$, the objective value is on average degraded by 56% to 21%, respectively.

The intensification is guaranteed by admitting enhanced solutions and by using the tabu search with a dynamic size of the tabu list to explore the neighborhoods. The characteristics of intensification and diversification of this tabu search are also presented in `Vns-Ts-MemExplorer`. If this approach uses a classic tabu search for the computational test, the solution cost is degraded by 35% on average.

7.2.3. *Approaches for dynamic memory allocation problem*

Two approaches have been proposed for this problem. As the long-term and the short-term approaches take advantage of metaheuristics designed for the previous memory allocation problem, its diversification and intensification are inherited from `Vns-Ts-MemExplorer`.

7.3. Conclusions

We summarize the main results of this chapter.

Addressing the first memory allocation problem has allowed us to introduce three new upper bounds on the chromatic number. These upper bounds do not make any assumption on the graph structure. From the theoretical and computational assessment, we have demonstrated the superiority of our bounds over the well-known bounds from the literature.

These upper bounds are easily computable even for large graphs. Indeed, there exist advanced bounds on the chromatic number, but they required a computational time longer than 20 minutes. It is far too long for the electronic chip designers, who must solve repeatedly the first version problem to do "what if" studies.

`Evo-Allocation` returns the best results for the second version of the memory allocation problem. This is due to its rigorous control of population diversity and a multi-parent crossover, as well as the variable size of the tabu list. `Vns-Ts-MemExplorer` reaches excellent results for the general memory allocation problem due to its two neighborhoods and the local search method (`TabuMemex`). The long-term approach achieves good results in a reasonable amount of time for the dynamic memory allocation problem. This is due to the approach taking into account the application requirements for the current and future time intervals.

We have shown that the results produced by our metaheuristics are better in terms of an objective function and running time than the results returned by the ILP and local search solvers. The success of metaheuristics designed for the memory allocation problems is due to their well-balanced search in terms of intensification and diversification.

The exact approach is suitable for today's applications; it is clearly not for tomorrow's needs. The proposed metaheuristics appear to be suitable for the needs of today and tomorrow. Moreover, the very modest CPU time compared to the exact method is an additional asset for integrating them to CAD tools, letting designers test different options in a reasonable amount of time.

The methods inspired by graph coloring problems can be successfully extended to more complex allocation problems for embedded systems, thereby assessing the gains made by using these methods to specific cases in terms of energy consumption. Moreover, the approaches designed for the version of memory allocation give promising perspectives for using metaheuristics in the field of electronic design. Thus, this shows that operations research can bring significant contributions to electronics.

7.4. Future works

The following theoretical and practical perspectives can be drawn from this chapter.

7.4.1. *Theoretical perspectives*

We can use more information on graph topology for producing competitive upper bounds for the chromatic number. Indeed, we have proposed three upper bounds based on the degree of saturation of vertices and on the number of vertices and edges. For example, we might consider the graph density to generate new upper bounds.

The general and dynamic memory allocation problems can be seen as a mix of the vertex coloring and the *bin packing* problems. The bin packing problem consists of packing a set of objects into a finite number of bins of limited capacity so as to minimize the number of bins used. In the memory allocation problem, the data structures represent the objects and the memory banks represent the bins. Hence, it could be interesting to adapt algorithms dedicated to the bin packing problem to our memory allocation problems.

A good perspective is the implementation of an algorithm based on the greedy algorithm proposed by Dantzig [DAN 57] to solve the *unbounded knapsack* problem. The knapsack problem is given a set of items, each with a weight and a value, determining which items to include in a knapsack such that the total weight is less than or equal to a given limit and the total value of the knapsack is maximized. The idea is to compute a ratio for each data structure that is equal to the number of accesses divided by the size of the data structure. Then, there is the allocation of data structures sorted by a decreasing ratio. Thus, the small data structures that are accessed more often by the processor are more likely to be allocated to memory banks, and the remaining data structures can be allocated to the external memory. In this way, the total access cost may be minimized.

Sometimes, the long-term approach is outperformed by the short-term approach, because the long-term approach ignores the potential for updating the solution at each iteration. Consequently, future work should concentrate on a mid-term approach to combine the benefits of both approaches. The main idea is weighting the requirements of each time interval; thus, future requirements are less and less weighted as they are far away from the current time interval. This allows the mid-term approach to move easily the data structure at the time intervals by taking into account the future needs of the application. In this approach, the first step is determining the appropriate weight coefficients at each time interval. The mid-term approach is similar to the long-term approach; it builds the interval solution from the parent solution, which is selected among two candidate solutions. The first solution is the parent solution for the previous interval and the second solution is the solution found by MemExplorer solved with the weighted requirements to the current interval to the last one. The solution associated with the minimum cost is selected as the parent solution.

Based on the characteristics of previous algorithms, we might design a global approach for the dynamic memory allocation problem that builds a solution for all time intervals or implement other sophisticated metaheuristics, for example the honey bee algorithm [TOV 04], which is inspired by the behavior of a honey bee colony involved in nectar collection; the ant colony algorithm [COL 91], which is based on the behavior of ants seeking a path between their colony and a source of food; the scatter search and path relinking [GLO 98, GLO 00], which are the evolutionary methods based on joining a solution based on generalized path constructions.

For the larger instances of the memory allocation problems, it is not possible to solve the ILP with the current solvers. However, the limit of metaheuristics is that they do not guarantee optimal solutions. Thus, it seems a good idea to design matheuristics [MAN 09, HAN 09] to address these problems because they combine metaheuristics and mathematical programming techniques.

7.4.2. *Practical perspectives*

The success of our approaches gives promising perspectives for using metaheuristics in the field of electronic design. For example, in the memory allocation problem with a small granularity, data structures are split into words and the objective is to allocate them to memory banks so as to minimize the total access time [CAT 98b]. Another interesting problem, where our approaches can be adapted, is the case of multi-port memories, and the conflict graph that extends with loops and hyperedges [CAT 98b]. Here, the conflicts can be between two or more data structures.

These metaheuristics can be suitable for the register allocation problem, where the goal is to find an allocation of scalars to registers which takes into account the conflicts between scalars and minimizes the number of registers. They can be adapted to scratchpad optimization, for determining which instructions can be located in the scrachtpad for a rapid access.

Our approaches might be successfully extended to the data binding problems discussed in Chapter 1, for example, in the memory partition problem for low energy, which consists of partitioning data structures into a fixed number of memory banks so as to minimize the interferences between data structures. Also, it can be extended to the problems where the capacity of memory banks is limited, and to problems that use an external memory to store data structures.

Bibliography

[ANG 05] ANGIOLINI F., BENINI L., CAPRARA A., "An efficient profile-based algorithm for scratchpad memory partitioning", *IEEE Transactions on CAD of Integrated Circuits and Systems*, vol. 24, no. 11, pp. 1660–1676, 2005.

[AOU 10a] AOUAD M.I., IDOUMGHAR L., SCHOTT R., ZENDRA O., "Reduction of energy consumption in embedded systems: a hybrid evolutionary algorithm", *Proceedings of the 3rd International Conference on Metaheuristics and Nature Inspired Computing*, vol. 95, Djerba, Tunisia, 27–31 October 2010.

[AOU 10b] AOUAD M.I., IDOUMGHAR L., SCHOTT R., ZENDRA O., "Sequential and distributed hybrid GA-SA algorithms for energy optimization in embedded systems", *Proceedings of the International Conference Applied Computing*, Timisoara, Roumania, pp. 167–174, 21–23 October 2010.

[AOU 10c] AOUAD M.I., SCHOTT R., ZENDRA O., "A Tabu search heuristic for scratch-pad memory management", *Proceedings of the International Conference on Software Engineering and Technology*, Rome, Italy, pp. 386–390, 28–30 April 2010.

[AOU 10d] AOUAD M.I., SCHOTT R., ZENDRA O., "Genetic heuristics for reducing memory energy consumption in embedded systems", *Proceedings of the 5th International Conference on Software Engineering and Data Technologies*, Athens, Greece, pp. 394–402, 22–24 July 2010.

[AOU 10e] AOUAD M.I., SCHOTT R., ZENDRA O., "Hybrid heuristics for optimizing energy consumption in embedded systems", *Proceedings of the 25th International Symposium on Computer and Information Sciences*, London, pp. 409–414, 22–24 September 2010.

[AVI 02] AVISSAR O., BARUA R., STEWART D., "An optimal memory allocation scheme for scratch-pad-based embedded systems", *ACM Transactions on Embedded Computing Systems*, vol. 1, no. 1, pp. 6–26, 2002.

[BAJ 97] BAJWA R., HIRAKI M., KOJIMA H., GORNY D., NITTA K., SHRIDHAR A., SEKI K., SASAKI K., "Instruction buffering to reduce power in processors for signal processing", *IEEE Transactions on Very Large Scale Integration (VLSI) Systems*, vol. 5, no. 4, pp. 417–424, 1997.

[BAL 88] BALAKRISHNAN M., MAJUMDAR A., BANERJI D., LINDERS J., MAJITHIA J., "Allocation of multiport memories in data path synthesis", *IEEE Transactions on Computer-Aided Design of Integrated Circuits and Systems*, vol. 7, no. 4, pp. 536–540, 1988.

[BAL 07] BALASA F., Z. H., LUICAN I., "Computation of storage requirements for multi-dimensional signal processing applications", *IEEE Transactions on Very Large Scale Integration (VLSI) Systems*, vol. 15, no. 4, pp. 447–460, 2007.

[BAL 08] BALASA F., KJELDSBERG P. G., VANDECAPPELLE A., PALKOVIC M., HU Q., ZHU H., CATTHOOR F., "Storage estimation and design space exploration methodologies for the memory management of signal processing applications", *Journal of Signal Processing Systems*, vol. 53, nos. 1–2, pp. 51–71, 2008.

[BAN 02] BANAKAR R., STEINKE S., LEE B.-S., BALAKRISHNAN M., MARWEDEL P., "Scratchpad memory: design alternative for cache on-chip memory in embedded systems", *Proceedings of the 10th International Symposium on Hardware/Software Codesign*, New York, pp. 73–78, 6–8 May 2002.

[BAR 06] BARR M., MASSA A., *Programming Embedded Systems: With C and GNU Development Tools*, 2nd ed., O'Reilly Media, 2006.

[BAT 94] BATTITI R., TECCHIOLLI G., "The reactive Tabu search", *Informs Journal on Computing*, vol. 6, no. 2, pp. 126–140, 1994.

[BEN 00a] BENINI L., MACII A., MACII E., PONCINO M., "Increasing energy efficiency of embedded systems by application-specific memory hierarchy generation", *IEEE Design and Test Computers*, vol. 17, no. 2, pp. 74–85, 2000.

[BEN 00b] BENINI L., MACII A., PONCINO M., "A recursive algorithm for low-power memory partitioning", *Proceedings of the International Symposium on Low Power Electronics and Design*, Rapallo, Italy, pp. 78–83, 26–27 July 2000.

[BEN 00c] BENINI L., MICHELI G., "System-level power optimization: techniques and tools", *ACM Transactions on Design Automation of Electronic Systems*, vol. 5, no. 2, pp. 115–192, 2000.

[BEN 02a] BENINI L., BRUNI D., MACII A., MACII E., "Hardware-assisted data compression for energy minimization in systems with embedded processors", *Proceedings of the Conference on Design, Automation and Test in Europe*, Washington, DC, pp. 449–453, 2002.

[BEN 02b] BENINI L., BRUNI D., RICCÒ B., MACII A., MACII E., "An adaptive data compression scheme for memory traffic minimization in processor-based systems", *Proceedings of IEEE International Symposium on Circuits and Systems.*, pp. 866–869, 2002.

[BEN 02c] BENINI L., MACCHIARULO L., MACII A., PONCINO M., "Layout-driven memory synthesis for embedded systems-on-chip", *IEEE Transactions on Very Large Scale Integration (VLSI) Systems*, vol. 10, no. 2, pp. 96–105, 2002.

[BES 04] BESBES H., JEBARA S. F., "A solution to reduce noise enhancement in pre-whitened LMS-type algorithms: the double direction adaptation", *Proceedings of the Control, Communications and Signal Processing*, pp. 717–720, 2004.

[BLA 05] BLACK P., "Greedy algorithm", *Dictionary of Algorithms and Data Structures*, U.S. National Institute of Standards and Technology, 2005.

[BLA 10] BLAZY S., ROBILLARD B., APPEL A., "Formal verification of coalescing graph-coloring register allocation", *Proceedings of the European Symposium On Programming*, Paphos, Cyprus, pp. 145–164, 2010.

[BRÉ 79] BRÉLAZ D., "New methods to color the vertices of a graph", *Communications of the Association of Computer Machinery*, vol. 22, no. 4, pp. 251–256, 1979.

[BRE 08] BRENNER U., STRUZYNA M., VYGEN J., "BonnPlace: placement of leading-edge chips by advanced combinatorial algorithms", *IEEE Transactions on Computer-Aided Design of Integrated Circuits and Systems*, vol. 27, no. 9, pp. 1607–1620, 2008.

[BRO 00] BROCKMEYER E., GHEZ C., BAETENS W., CATTHOOR F., "Low-power processor-level data transfer and storage exploration", *European Low Power Initiative for electronic system Design. Unified low-power design flow for data-dominated multimedia and telecom applications*, Kluwer Academic Publishers, Dordrecht, pp. 26–63, 2000.

[BUI 08] BUI T., NGUYEN T., PATEL C., PHAN K., "An ant-based algorithm for coloring graphs", *Discrete Applied Mathematics*, vol. 156, no. 2, pp. 190–200, 2008.

[CAR 66] CARLSON R., NEMHAUSER G., "Scheduling to minimize interaction cost", *Operations Research*, vol. 14, no. 1, pp. 52–58, 1966.

[CAR 08] CARAMIA M., DELL'OLMO P., "Coloring graphs by iterated local search traversing feasible and infeasible solutions", *Discrete Applied Mathematics*, vol. 156, no. 2, pp. 201–217, 2008.

[CAT 94] CATTHOOR F., FRANSSEN F., WUYTACK S., NACHTERGAELE L., DE MAN H., "Global communication and memory optimizing transformations for low power signal processing systems", *Proceedings of the VLSI Signal Processing, VII*, pp. 178–187, 1994.

[CAT 98a] CATTHOOR F., JANSSEN M., NACHTERGAELE L., DE MAN H., "System-level data-flow transformation exploration and power-area trade-offs demonstrated on video coders", *The Journal of VLSI Signal Processing*, vol. 18, no. 1, pp. 39–50, 1998.

[CAT 98b] CATTHOOR F., WUYTACK S., DE GREEF E., F.B., NACHTERGAELE L., VANDECAPPELLE A., *Custom Memory Management Methodology*, Kluwer Academic Publishers, 1998.

[CAT 98c] CATTHOOR F., WUYTACK S., DE GREEF E., FRANSSEN F., NACHTERGAELE L., DE MAN H., "System-level transformations for low power data transfer and storage", *Proceedings of the Low-Power CMOS Design*, Monastir, Tunisia, pp. 609–618, 1998.

[CAT 01] CATTHOOR F., DANCKAERT K., WUYTACK S., DUTT N., "Code transformations for data transfer and storage exploration preprocessing in multimedia processors", *IEEE Design and Test computers*, vol. 18, no. 3, pp. 70–82, 2001.

[CHA 95] CHANDRAKASAN A., POTKONJAK M., MEHRA R., RABAEY J., BRODERSEN R., "Optimizing power using transformations", *IEEE Transactions on Computer-Aided Design of Integrated Circuits and Systems*, vol. 14, no. 1, pp. 12–31, 1995.

[CHA 04] CHAITIN G., "Register allocation and spilling via graph coloring", *SIGPLAN Notices*, vol. 39, no. 4, pp. 66–74, 2004.

[CHA 09] CHANG Y.-W., JIANG Z.-W., CHEN T.-C., "Essential issues in analytical placement algorithms", *Information and Media Technologies*, vol. 4, no. 4, pp. 815–836, 2009.

[CHI 02] CHIMIENTIA A., FANUCCI L., LOCATELLIC R., SAPONARAC S., "VLSI architecture for a low-power video codec system", *Microelectronics Journal*, vol. 33, no. 5, pp. 417–427, 2002.

[CHI 07] CHIARANDINI M., PAQUETE, PREUSS M., RIDGE E., Experiments on metaheuristics: methodological overview and open issues, Report no. DMF-2007-03-003, The Danish Mathematical Society, Denmark, 2007.

[CHO 09] CHO D., PASRICHA S., ISSENIN I., DUTT N., AHN M., PAEK Y., "Adaptive scratch pad memory management for dynamic behavior of multimedia applications", *Transactions on Computer-Aided Design of Integrated Circuits and Systems*, vol. 28, no. 4, pp. 554–567, 2009.

[COJ 06] COJA-OGHLAN A., KUHTZ L., "An improved algorithm for approximating the chromatic number of Gn,p", *Information Processing Letters*, vol. 99, no. 6, pp. 234–238, 2006.

[COL 91] COLORNI A., DORIGO M., MANIEZZO V., "Distributed optimization by ant colonies", *Proceedings of European Conference on Artificial Life*, Paris, France, pp. 134–142, 1991.

[CON 99] CONOVER W. J., *Practical Nonparametric Statistic*, 3rd ed., Wiley, New York, 1999.

[CON 09] CONG J., JIANG W., LIU B., ZOU Y., "Automatic memory partitioning and scheduling for throughput and power optimization", *Proceedings of the IEEE/ACM International Conference on Computer-Aided Design – Digest of Technical Papers*, ACM, New York, pp. 697–704, 2–5 November 2009.

[COR 90] CORMEN T., LEISERSON C., RIVEST R., STEIN C., "Greedy Algorithms", in *Introduction to Algorithms*, 2nd ed., The Massachusetts Institute of Technology, pp. 370–404, 1990.

[COR 10] CORVINO R., GAMATIÉ A., BOULET P., "Architecture exploration for efficient data transfer and storage in data-parallel applications", *Proceedings of the 16th International Euro-Par Conference on Parallel Processing: Part I*, Berlin, Heidelberg, pp. 101–116, 2010.

[COU 06] COUSSY P., CASSEAU E., BOMEL P., BAGANNE A., MARTIN E., "A formal method for hardware IP design and integration under I/O and timing constraints", *ACM Transactions on Embedded Computing System*, vol. 5, no. 1, pp. 29–53, 2006.

[COU 09] COUSSY P., ROSSI A., SEVAUX M., SÖRENSEN K., TRABELSI K., "VNS for high-level synthesis", *Proceedings of 8th Metaheuristics International Conference*, MIC 2009, Hamburg, Germany, pp. 173:1–173:10, 2009.

[CRÉ 10] CRÉPUT J.-C., DAFALI R., ROSSI A., SEVAUX M., ZERBO B., "From simple heuristics to evolutionary approach for routing messages in a NoC", *Proceedings of 10th Anniversary of the Metaheuristic Community*, Lorient, France, pp. 55–57, 2010.

[CUP 98] CUPAK M., KULKARNI C., CATTHOOR F., DE MAN H., "Functional validation of system-level loop transformations for power efficient caching", *Proceedings of the Workshop on System Design Automation*, Dresden, Germany, 30–31 March 1998.

[CUT 08] CUTCUTACHE I., WONG W.-F., "Fast, frequency-based, integrated register allocation and instruction scheduling", *Software: Practice and Experience*, vol. 38, no. 11, pp. 1105–1126, 2008.

[DAF 08] DAFALI R., DIGUET J.-P., SEVAUX M., "Key research issues for reconfigurable Network-on-Chip", *Proceedings of the International Conference on ReConFigurable Computing and FPGAs, ReConFig'08*, Cancun, Mexico, pp. 181–186, 2008.

[DAN 57] DANTZIG G. B., "Discrete-variable extremum problems", *Operations Research*, vol. 5, no. 2, pp. 266–288, 1957.

[DEG 95] DE GREEF E., CATTHOOR F., DE MAN H., "Mapping real-time motion estimation type algorithms to memory efficient, programmable multi-processor architectures", *Microprocessing and Microprogramming*, vol. 41, nos. 5-6, pp. 409–423, 1995. [Parallel programmable architectures and compilation.]

[DEG 97] DE GREEF E., CATTHOOR F., DE MAN H., "Memory size reduction through storage order optimization for embedded parallel multimedia applications", *Proceedings of Workshop on Parallel Processing and Multimedia*, Geneva, Switzerland, pp. 84–98, 1997.

[DIE 05] DIESTEL R., *Graph Theory*, vol. 173 of *Graduate Texts in Mathematics*, Springer-Verlag, Heidelberg, 2005.

[DIM 11] DIMACS, 2011, available at http://mat.gsia.cmu.edu/COLOR/instances.html.

[DU 08] DU X., LI Z., GAO X., YAN L., "Optimizing the performance of chip shooter machine based on improved genetic algorithm", *Proceedings of the 7th World Congress on Intelligent Control and Automation*, Chongqing, China, pp. 2849–2853, 2008.

[EGG 08] EGGER B., LEE J., SHIN H., "Dynamic scratchpad memory management for code in portable systems with an MMU", *ACM Transactions on Embedded Computing Systems*, vol. 7, no. 2, pp. 11:1–11:38, 2008.

[FAR 95] FARRAHI A., TÉLLEZ G., SARRAFZADEH M., "Memory segmentation to exploit sleep mode operation", *Proceedings of the 32nd annual ACM/IEEE Design Automation Conference*, New York, pp. 36–41, 1995.

[FIC 09] FICO, "Xpress-MP", 2009, available at http://www.dashoptimization.com/.

[FRA 94] FRANSSEN F., NACHTERGAELE L., SAMSOM H., CATTHOOR F., DE MAN H., "Control flow optimization for fast system simulation and storage minimization [real-time multidimensional signal processing]", *Proceedings of the European Conference on Design Automation*, Paris, France, pp. 20–24, 1994.

[FRA 04] FRANCESCO P., MARCHAL P., ATIENZA D., BENINI L., CATTHOOR F., MENDIAS J., "An integrated hardware/software approach for run-time scratchpad management", *Proceedings of the 41st annual Design Automation Conference*, New York, pp. 238–243, 2004.

[FRI 37] FRIEDMAN M., "The use of ranks to avoid the assumption of normality implicit in the analysis of variance", *Journal of the American Statistical Association*, vol. 32, pp. 675–701, 1937.

[GAJ 92] GAJSKI D., DUTT N., WU A., LIN S., *High-Level synthesis: Introduction to Chip and System Design*, Kluwer Academic Publishers, Norwell, MA, 1992.

[GAL 99] GALINIER P., HAO J.-K., "Hybrid evolutionary algorithms for graph coloring", *Journal of Combinatorial Optimization*, vol. 3, pp. 379–397, 1999.

[GAR 79] GAREY M., JOHNSON D., *Computers and Intractability; A Guide to the Theory of NP-Completeness*, W. H. Freeman & Co., New York, 1979.

[GAU 93] GAUT, "High-level synthesis tool", 1993, available at http://hls-labsticc.univ-ubs.fr/.

[GLO 97] GLOVER F., LAGUNA M., *Tabu Search*, Kluwer Academic Publisher, Dordrecht, The Netherlands, 1997.

[GLO 98] GLOVER F., "A template for scatter search and path relinking", *Proceedings of the 3rd European Conference, Artificial evolution*, vol. 1363, Nîmes, France, pp. 13–54, 1998.

[GLO 00] GLOVER F., LAGUNA M., MARTÍ R., "Fundamentals of scatter search and path relinking", *Control and Cybernetics*, vol. 39, pp. 653–684, 2000.

[GNU 09] GNU, GLPK Linear Programming Kit, 2009, available at http://www.gnu.org/software/glpk/.

[GON 96] GONZALEZ R., HOROWITZ M., "Energy dissipation in general purpose microprocessors", *IEEE Journal of Solid-State Circuits*, vol. 31, no. 9, pp. 1277–1284, 1996.

[GON 02] GONZÁLEZ-VELARDE J.-L., LAGUNA M., "Tabu search with simple ejection chains for coloring graphs", *Annals of Operations Research*, vol. 117, no. 1, pp. 165–174, 2002.

[GRA 11] Graph coloring, 2011, available at http://en.wikipedia.org/wiki /Graph_coloring.

[GRU 07] GRUND D., HACK S., "A fast cutting-plane algorithm for optimal coalescing", *Proceedings of the 16th International Conference on Compiler Construction*, Berlin, Heidelberg, pp. 111–125, 2007.

[HAN 09] HANSEN P., MANIEZZO V., VOSSS., "Special issue on mathematical contributions to metaheuristics editorial", *Journal of Heuristics*, vol. 15, no. 3, pp. 197–199, 2009.

[HEA 03] HEATH S., *Embedded Systems Design*, 2nd ed., EDN series for design engineers, Elsevier, 2003.

[HEL 03] HELD S., KORTE B., MASSERG J., RINGE M., VYGEN J., "Clock scheduling and clocktree construction for high performance ASICS", *Proceedings of the 2003 IEEE/ACM International Conference on Computer-Aided Design*, Washington, DC, pp. 232–239, 2003.

[HEN 07] HENNESSY J., PATTERSON D., *Computer Architecture, a Quantitative Approach*, 4th ed., Morgan Kaufmann, San Francisco, CA, 2007.

[HER 87] HERZ A., DE WERRA D., "Using tabu search techniques for graph coloring", *Computing*, vol. 39, no. 4, pp. 345–351, 1987.

[HER 08] HERTZ A., PLUMETTAZ M., ZUFFEREY N., "Variable space search for graph coloring", *Discrete Applied Mathematics*, vol. 156, no. 13, pp. 2551–2560, 2008.

[HUA 09] HUANG S.-H., CHENG C.-H., "Minimum-period register binding", *IEEE Transactions on Computer-Aided Design of Integrated Circuits and Systems*, vol. 28, no. 8, pp. 1265–1269, 2009.

[IDO 10] IDOUMGHAR L., IDRISSI AOUAD M., MELKEMI M., SCHOTT R., "Metropolis particle swarm optimization algorithm with mutation operator for global optimization problems", *Proceedings of the 22th International Conference on Tools with Artificial Intelligence*, Arras, France, pp. 35–42, 2010.

[INN 10] E-LAB INNOVATION & OPTIMISATION B., "LocalSolver 1.0", 2010, available at http://e-lab.bouygues.com/?p=693.

[ISS 07] ISSENIN I., BROCKMEYER E., MIRANDA M., DUTT N., "DRDU: a data reuse analysis technique for efficient scratch-pad memory management", *ACM Transactions on Design Automation of Electronic Systems*, vol. 12, no. 2, ACM, New York, April 2007.

[IVE 99] IVERSON M., OZGUNER F., POTTER L., "Statistical prediction of task execution times through analytic benchmarking for scheduling in a heterogeneous environment", *IEEE Transactions on Computers*, vol. 48, no. 12, pp. 1374–1379, 1999.

[KAM 08] KAMAL R., *Embedded Systems. Architecture, Programming and Design*, 2nd ed., Tata McGraw-Hill, 2008.

[KAN 05] KANDEMIR M., IRWIN M., CHEN G., KOLCU I., "Compiler-guided leakage optimization for banked scratch-pad memories", *IEEE Transactions on Very Large Scale Integration (VLSI) Systems*, vol. 13, no. 10, pp. 1136–1146, 2005.

[KAR 72] KARP R., "Reducibility amongcombinatorial problems", *Complexity of Computer Computation*, pp. 85–103, 1972.

[KHA 09] KHAN S., SHIN H., "Effective memory access optimization by memory delay modeling, memory allocation, and buffer allocation", *Proceedings of the International SoC Design Conference*, Busan, Korea, pp. 153–156, 2009.

[KIE 11] KIEFFER Y., "Recherche opérationnelle pour la CAO micro-électronique", *GDR-RO micro-électronique*, 2011.

[KLO 02] KLOTZ W., Graph coloring algorithms, Report, Mathematik-Bericht, Clausthal University of Technology, Clausthal, Germany, 2002.

[KNU 94] KNUTH D.E., "The Sandwich Theorem", *The Electronic Journal of Combinatorics*, vol. 1, no. 1, pp. 1–49, 1994.

[KOE 06] KOES D.R., GOLDSTEIN S.C., An analysis of graph coloring register allocation, Report no. CMU-CS-06-111, Carnegie Mellon University, March 2006.

[KOE 09] KOES D.R., GOLDSTEIN S.C., "Register allocation deconstructed", *Proceedings of the 12th International Workshop on Software and Compilers for Embedded Systems*, New York, pp. 21–30, 2009.

[KOL 94] KOLSON D., NICOLAU A., DUTT N., "Minimization of memory traffic in high-level synthesis", *Proceedings of the 31st Conference on Design Automation*, San Diego, CA, pp. 149–154, 1994.

[KOL 95] KOLEN A., LENSTRA J., Chapter "Combinatorics in operations research", *Handbook of Combinatorics*, Elsevier Science, Amsterdam, The Netherlands, pp. 1875–1910, 1995.

[KOR 04] KORANNE S., "A note on system-on-chip test scheduling formulation", *Journal of Electronic Testing*, vol. 20, no. 3, pp. 309–313, 2004.

[KOR 08] KORTE B., VYGEN J., "Combinatorial problems in chip design", in TÓTH G.F., KATONA G.O.H., LOVÁSZ L., PÁLFY P.P., RECSKI A., STIPSICZ A., SZÁSZ D., MIKLÓS D.O., GRÖTSCHEL M., KATONA G.O.H., SGI G. (eds), *Building Bridges*, vol. 19 of *Bolyai Society Mathematical Studies*, Springer Berlin Heidelberg, pp. 333–368, 2008.

[KUM 07] KUMAR T.R., RAVIKUMAR C., GOVINDARAJAN R., "MAX: a multi objective memory architecture eXploration framework for embedded systems-on-chip", *Proceedings of the 20th International Conference on VLSI Design* held jointly with *6th International Conference on Embedded Systems*, Bangalore, India, pp. 527–533, 2007.

[KUR 87] KURDAHI F.J., PARKER A.C., "REAL: a program for REgister ALlocation", *Proceedings of the 24th ACM / IEEE Design Automation Conference*, New York, pp. 210–215, 1987.

[LAB 06] LAB-STICC, Soft Explorer, 2006, available at http://www.softexplorer.fr/.

[LAB 11] LAB-STICC, 2011, available at http://www.lab-sticc.fr/.

[LAC 03] LACOMME P., PRINS C., SEVAUX M., *Algorithmes de graphes*, Eyrolles, 2003.

[LEE 02] LEE W., CHANG M., "A study of dynamic memory management in C++ programs", *Computer Languages Systems and Structures*, vol. 28, no. 3, pp. 237–272, 2002.

[LIP 93] LIPPENS P., VAN MEERBERGEN J., VERHAEGH W., VAN DER WERF A., "Allocation of multiport memories for hierarchical data streams", *Proceedings of the International Conference on Computer-Aided Design*, IEEE/ACM, Santa Clara CA, pp. 728–735, 1993.

[LUI 07a] LUICAN I., ZHU H., BALASA F., "Mapping model with inter-array memory sharing for multidimensional signal processing", *Proceedings of the IEEE/ACM International Conference on Computer-Aided Design*, Piscataway, NJ, pp. 160–165, 2007.

[LUI 07b] LUICAN I., ZHU H., BALASA F., "Signal-to-memory mapping analysis for multimedia signal processing", *Proceedings of the 2007 Asia and South Pacific Design Automation Conference*, Washington, DC, pp. 486–491, 2007.

[MÉN 08] MÉNDEZ-DÍAZ I., ZABALA P., "A cutting plane algorithm for graph coloring", *Discrete Applied Mathematics*, vol. 156, no. 2, pp. 159–179, 2008.

[MAC 05] MACCI A., "Memory organization for low-energy embedded systems", *Low-Power Electronics Design*, Computer Engineering Series, CRC Press LLC, pp. 26:1–26:12, 2005.

[MAH 09] MAHAJAN A., ALI M., "Hybrid evolutionary algorithm for the graph coloring register allocation problem for embedded systems", *Transactions on Computational Science V*, vol. 5540 of *Lecture Notes in Computer Science*, Springer Berlin / Heidelberg, pp. 206–219, 2009.

[MAN 09] MANIEZZO V., STÜTZLE T., VOSS S., *Matheuristics: Hybridizing Metaheuristics and Mathematical Programming*, vol. 10 of *Annals of information systems*, Springer, New York, 2009.

[MAR 03] MARKOVSKIY Y., *Distributed Memory Allocation Problem*, 2003, available at http://www.eng.ucy.ac.cy/theocharides/Courses/ECE656/memory_problem.pdf.

[MAR 10a] MARCHETTI O., Problématiques d'optimisation discrète en micro-électronique, GDR-RO micro-électronique, 2010.

[MAR 10b] MARCHETTI O., Synthèse du projet problématiques d'optimisation discrète en micro-électronique, GDR-RO micro-électronique, 2010.

[MAS 99] MASSELOS K., CATTHOOR F., GOUTIS C., DEMAN H., "A performance-oriented use methodology of power optimizing code transformations for multimedia applications realized on programmable multimedia processors", *Proceedings of the IEEE Workshop on Signal Processing Systems*, Taipei, Taiwan, pp. 261–270, 1999.

[MEH 96] MEHROTRA A., TRICK M., "A column generation approach for graph coloring", *INFORMS Journal on Computing*, vol. 8, no. 4, pp. 344–354, 1996.

[MEN 95] MENG T., GORDON B., TSERN E., HUNG A., "Portable video-on-demand in wireless communication", *Proceedings of the IEEE*, vol. 83, no. 4, pp. 659–680, 1995.

[MLA 97] MLADENOVIĆ N., HANSEN P., "Variable neighbourhood decomposition search", *Computers and Operations Research*, vol. 24, no. 11, pp. 1097–1100, 1997.

[MUR 08] MURRAY A., FRANKE B., "Fast source-level data assignment to dual memory banks", *Proceedings of the 11th International Workshop on Software and Compilers for Embedded Systems*, New York, pp. 43–52, 2008.

[NAC 96] NACHTERGAELE L., CATTHOOR F., KAPOOR B., JANSSENS S., MOOLENAAR D., "Low power storage exploration for H.263 video decoder", *Proceedings VLSI Signal Processing, IX*, San Francisco, California, pp. 115–124, October 1996.

[NAC 01] NACHTERGAELE L., CATTHOOR F., KULKARNI C., "Random-access data storage components in customized architectures", *Design Test of Computers, IEEE*, vol. 18, no. 3, pp. 40–54, 2001.

[NAM 04] NAMHOON K., PENG R., "A memory allocation assignment method using multiway partitioning", *Proceedings of the Conference*, Newtonmore, Scotland, pp. 143–144, 2004.

[NOE 05] NOERGAARD T., *Embedded Systems Architecture*, Embedded Technology, Elsevier, 2005.

[OZT 09] OZTURK O., KANDEMIR M., IRWIN M., "Using data compression for increasing memory system utilization", *IEEE Transactions on Computer-Aided Design of Integrated Circuits and Systems*, vol. 28, no. 6, pp. 901–914, 2009.

[PAN 97a] PANDA P., DUTT N., NICOLAU A., "Architectural exploration and optimization of local memory in embedded systems", *Proceedings of the 10th International Symposium on System Synthesis*, Antwerp, Belgium, pp. 90–97, 17–19 September 1997.

[PAN 97b] PANDA P., DUTT N., NICOLAU A., "Efficient utilization of scratch-pad memory in embedded processor applications", *Proceedings of the European Design and Test Conference*, Paris, France, pp. 7–11, 1997.

[PAN 99] PANDA P., NICOLAU A., DUTT N., *Memory Issues in Embedded Systems-on-Chip: Optimizations and Exploration*, Kluwer Academic Publishers, Hingham, MA, 1999.

[PAN 00] PANDA P., DUTT N., NICOLAU A., "On-chip vs. off-chip memory: the data partitioning problem in embedded processor-based systems", *ACM Transactions on Design Automation of Electronic Systems*, vol. 5, no. 3, pp. 682–704, 2000.

[PAN 01a] PANDA P., DUTT N., NICOLAU A., CATTHOOR F., VANDECAPPELLE A., BROCKMEYER E., KULKARNI C., DE GREEF E., "Data Memory Organization and Optimizations in Application-Specific Systems", *IEEE Design & Test of Computers*, vol. 18, no. 3, pp. 56–68, 2001.

[PAN 01b] PANDA P.R., CATTHOOR F., DUTT N.D., DANCKAERT K., BROCKMEYER E., KULKARNI C., VANDERCAPPELLE A., KJELDSBERG P.G., "Data and memory optimization techniques for embedded systems", *ACM Transactions on Design Automation of Electronic Systems*, vol. 6, no. 2, pp. 149–206, 2001.

[PER 08] PEREIRA Q., F. M., JENS P., "Register allocation by puzzle solving", *SIGPLAN Not*, vol. 43, no. 6, pp. 216–226, 2008.

[PEY 09] PEYER S., RAUTENBACH D., VYGEN J., "A generalization of Dijkstra's shortest path algorithm with applications to VLSI routing", *Journal of Discrete Algorithms*, vol. 7, no. 4, pp. 377–390, 2009.

[PIN 93] PINTER S., "Register allocation with instruction scheduling", *SIGPLAN Notices*, vol. 28, no. 6, pp. 248–257, 1993.

[POR 09a] PORUMBEL D., "DIMACS graphs: benchmark instances and best upper bound", 2009, available at http://www.info.univ-angers.fr/pub/porumbel/graphs/.

[POR 09b] PORUMBEL D., HAO J.-K., KUNTZ. P., "Diversity control and multi-parent recombination for evolutionary graph coloring algorithms", *Proceedings of the 9th Conference on Evolutionay Computation in Combinatorial Optimization*, Tübingen, Germany, pp. 121–132, 2009.

[POR 10] PORUMBEL D., HAO J.-K., KUNTZ P., "A search space cartography for guiding graph coloring heuristics", *Computers and Operations Research*, vol. 37, no. 4, pp. 769–778, 2010.

[RAB 02] RABAEY J., CHANDRAKASAN A., NIKOLIC B., *Digital Integrated Circuits: A Design Perspective*, 2nd ed., Prentice-Hall, 2002.

[RAM 05] RAMACHANDRAN A., JACOME M., "Xtream-fit: an energy-delay efficient data memory subsystem for embedded media processing", *IEEE Transactions on Computer-Aided Design of Integrated Circuits and Systems*, vol. 24, no. 6, pp. 832–848, 2005.

[REG 04] REGO C., GLOVER F., "Local search and metaheuristics", in DU D.-Z., PARDALOS P. M., GUTIN G., PUNNEN A., (eds), *The Traveling Salesman Problem and Its Variations*, vol. 12 of *Combinatorial Optimization*, Springer pp. 309–368, 2004.

[ROS 08] ROSSI A., SEVAUX M., "Mixed-integer linear programming formulation for High Level Synthesis", *Proceedings of the 11th International Workshop on Project Management and Scheduling*, PMS 2008, Istanbul, Turkey, pp. 222–226, 2008.

[SCH 92] SCHÖNFELD M., SCHWIEGERSHAUSEN M., PIRSCH P., "Synthesis of intermediate memories for the data supply to processor arrays", *Proceedings of the International Workshop on Algorithms and Parallel VLSI Architectures II*, Amsterdam, The Netherlands, pp. 365–370, 1992.

[SEN 09] SENN E., MONNEREAU D., ROSSI A., JULIEN N., "Using integer linear programming in test-bench generation for evaluating communication processors", *Proceedings of the 2009 12th Euromicro Conference on Digital System Design, Architectures, Methods and Tools*, Washington, DC, pp. 217–220, 2009.

[SEV 11] SEVAUX M., SINGH A., ROSSI A., "Tabu search for multiprocessor scheduling: application to high level synthesis", *Asia-Pacific Journal of Operational Research*, vol. 28, no. 2, pp. 201–212, 2011.

[SHE 07] SHENGNING W., SIKUN L., "Extending traditional graph-coloring register allocation exploiting meta-heuristics for embedded systems", *Proceedings of the 3rd International Conference on Natural Computation*, Haikou, China, pp. 324–329, 2007.

[SHI 93] SHIN H., KIM C., "A simple yet effective technique for partitioning", *IEEE Transactions on Very Large Scale Integration Systems*, vol. 1, no. 3, pp. 380–386, 1993.

[SHY 07] SHYAM K., GOVINDARAJAN R., "An array allocation scheme for energy reduction in partitioned memory architectures", *Proceedings of the 16th International Conference on Compiler Construction*, Berlin, Heidelberg, pp. 32–47, 2007.

[SIN 03] SINGH M., PRASANNA V., "Algorithmic techniques for memory energy reduction", *Proceedings of the 2nd International Conference on Experimental and Efficient Algorithms*, Berlin, Heidelberg, pp. 237–252, 2003.

[SIP 03] SIPKOVÀ V., "Efficient variable allocation to dual memory banks of DSPs", *Proceedings of the 7th International Workshop on Software and Compilers for Embedded Systems*, Vienna, Austria, pp. 359–372, 2003.

[SLO 97] SLOCK P., WUYTACK S., CATTHOOR F., JONG G., "Fast and extensive system-level memory exploration for ATM applications", *Proceedings of the 10th International Symposium on System Synthesis*, Anthwerp, Belgium, pp. 74–81, 1997.

[SÖR 03] SÖRENSEN K., A framework for robust and flexible optimization using metaheuristics, PhD Thesis, Universiteit Antwerpen, 2003.

[SOT 09] SOTO M., ROSSI A., SEVAUX M., "Two upper bounds on the chromatic number", *Proceedings of 8th Cologne-Twente Workshop on Graphs and Combinatorial Optimization*, Paris, France, pp. 191–194, 2009.

[SOT 10] SOTO M., ROSSI A., SEVAUX M., "Métaheuristiques pour l'allocation de mémoire dans les systèmes embarqués", *Proceedings of the 11e congrès de la société Française de Recherche Opérationnelle et d'Aide à la Décision*, Toulouse, France, pp. 35–43, 2010.

[SOT 11a] SOTO M., ROSSI A., SEVAUX M., "A mathematical model and a metaheuristic approach for a memory allocation problem", *Journal of Heuristics*, Springer, The Netherlands, pp. 1–19, 2011.

[SOT 11b] SOTO M., ROSSI A., SEVAUX M., "Three new upper bounds on the chromatic number", *Discrete Applied Mathematics*, vol. 159, no.18, pp. 2281–2289, 2011.

[SOT 11c] SOTO M., ROSSI A., SEVAUX M., "Two iterative metaheuristic approaches to dynamic memory allocation for embedded systems", in MERZ P., HAO J.-K. (eds), *Evolutionary Computation in Combinatorial Optimization*, vol. 6622 of *Lecture Notes in Computer Science*, Springer, Berlin/Heidelberg, pp. 250–261, 2011.

[STA 01] STACHO L., "New upper bounds for the chromatic number of a graph", *Journal of Graph Theory*, vol. 36, no. 2, pp. 117–120, 2001.

[STA 02] STACHO L., "A note on upper bound for the chromatic number of a graph", *Acta Mathematica Universitatis Comenianae*, vol. 71, no. 1, pp. 1–2, 2002.

[STE 02] STEINKE S., WEHMEYER L., LEE B., MARWEDEL P., "Assigning program and data objects to scratchpad for energy reduction", *Proceedings of the Conference on Design, Automation and Test in Europe*, Washington DC, pp. 409–415, 2002.

[STO 92] STOK L., JESS J.A.G., "Foreground memory management in data path synthesis", *International Journal of Circuit Theory and Applications*, vol. 20, no. 3, pp. 235–255, 1992.

[TIW 94] TIWARI V., MALIK S., WOLFE A., "Power analysis of embedded software: a first step towards software power minimization", *IEEE Transactions on Very Large Scale Integration (VLSI) Systems*, vol. 2, no. 4, pp. 437–445, 1994.

[TOP 07] TOPCUOGLU H., DEMIROZ B., KANDEMIR M., "Solving the register allocation problem for embedded systems using a hybrid evolutionary algorithm", *Evolutionary Computation*, vol. 11, no. 5, pp. 620–634, 2007.

[TOV 04] TOVEY C., "Honey bee algorithm: a biologically inspired approach to internet server optimization", *Engineering Enterprise: The Alumni Magazine for ISyE at Georgia Institute of Technology*, Spring, pp. 13–15, 2004.

[TRA 08] TRABELSI K., COUSSY P., ROSSI A., SEVAUX M., "Ordonnancement et Assignation en Synthèse de Haut Niveau", *Congrès de la Société Française de Recherche Opérationnelle et d'Aide à la Décision*, Clermont-Ferrand, France, 2008.

[TRA 10] TRABELSI K., SEVAUX M., COUSSY P., ROSSI A., SÖRENSEN K., "Advanced metaheuristics, for high-level synthesis", *Metaheuristics* Springer, Berlin, 2010.

[TRO 02] TRONÇON R., BRUYNOOGHE M., JANSSENS G., CATTHOOR F., "Storage size reduction by in-place mapping of arrays", *Proceedings of the 3rd International Workshop on Verification, Model Checking, and Abstract Interpretation*, London, pp. 167–181, 2002.

[TSE 86] TSENG C., SIEWIOREK D., "Automated synthesis of data paths in digital systems", *IEEE Transactions on Computer-Aided Design of Integrated Circuits and Systems*, vol. 5, no. 3, pp. 379–395, 1986.

[VER 91] VERBAUWHEDE I., CATTHOOR F., VANDEWALLE J., MAN H., "In-place memory management of algebraic algorithms on application specific ICs", *The Journal of VLSI Signal Processing*, vol. 3, no. 3, pp. 193–200, 1991.

[VER 04] VERMA M., WEHMEYER L., MARWECLEL P., "Dynamic overlay of scratchpad memory for energy minimization", *Proceedings of the International Conference on Hardware/Software Codesign and System Synthesis*, Washington DC, pp. 104–109, 2004.

[VRE 03] VREDEVELD T., LENSTRA J., "On local search for the generalized graph coloring problem", *Operations Research Letters*, vol. 31, no. 1, pp. 28–34, 2003.

[WEL 67] WELSH D. J.A., POWELL M.B., "An upper bound for the chromatic number of a graph and its application to timetabling problems", *The Computer Journal*, vol. 10, no. 1, pp. 85–86, 1967.

[WUY 96] WUYTACK S., CATTHOOR F., NACHTERGAELE L., DE MAN H., "Power exploration for data dominated video applications", *Proceedings of the International Symposium on Low Power Electronics and Design*, Monterey, CA, pp. 359–364, 1996.

[XIK 07] XIKUI L., YAN L., "Efficient DNA algorithms for chromatic number of graph problems", *Proceedings of the IEEE International Conference on Automation and Logistics*, Jinan, China, pp. 450–454, 2007.

[ZEI 04] ZEITLHOFER T., WESS B., "A comparison of graph coloring heuristics for register allocation based on coalescing in interval graphs", *Proceedings of the International Symposium on Circuits and Systems*, Vancouver, Canada, pp. 529–32, 2004.

[ZHA 11] ZHANG L., QIU M., SHA E., ZHUGE Q., "Variable assignment and instruction scheduling for processor with multi-module memory", *Microprocessors and Microsystems*, vol. 35, no. 3, pp. 308–317, 2011.

Index

M

mapping, 13, 14
MemExplorer, 131-144
memory conflict graph
(MCG), 131, 143-139
memory management-
memory allocation
problem-memory bank,
memory architecture-
memory partitioning, 1-25

N, O

neighborhood, 91-93
on-chip memory bank
capacity, 132
optimization technique,
8-21

P

parsing yield, 133
power consumption, 4-8

power performance, 4-8
proposal metaheuristic,
65-71, 85-94

R, S, T

register allocation, 15
scratchpad memory (SPM),
14
software, 9-11
tabu search procedure,
66-69, 89-91

V

variable neighborhood
search (VNS), 19, 77,
3-94
vertex coloring problem,
12